Real I

Dear Christina,

Enjoy reading this book!

Belinda G.

2.2.'24.

Belinda Ginns

Copyright © 2023 *Belinda Ginns*

All Rights Reserved

Dedication 奉獻

I'd like to dedicate this book to my four boys: Andrew, Harry, Samuel and Thomas, who are growing up to be great men! This book is also dedicated to James, my hubby and friend, who has supported me all the way. Thank you guys! I love you all!

I'd also like to thank my lovely sister Heidi Leung, whose Cantonese translation is just perfect! You're talented sis! I couldn't have done it without you!

However, ultimately I'd like to thank my precious Heavenly Father, who watches over me and blesses my life to overflowing. ~

~我謹將本書獻給我的四個兒子：Andrew、Harry、Samuel 和 Thomas，他們會成長為偉大的男人的！也獻給我的丈夫和朋友 James - 他一直支持我。感謝你們！我愛你們！

我還要感謝我親愛的妹妹 Heidi Leung，她的廣東話翻譯簡直太完美了！妹，你做得太好了！沒有你我不可能出到這本書！

然而，最終我要感謝我親愛的天父，祂看顧我並祝福我的生命直到豐盛滿溢。~

About the Author

Belinda Ginns, B.Ed., TOSEL, has more than 20 years of experience as an English Lecturer in Hong Kong. She has taught in different corporations, schools, vocational training centres, and tertiary educational institutions in Hong Kong, including The City University and The University of Science and Technology. She was also involved in the facilitation of translation and communication in the area of personnel development at Cathay Pacific Airways. Being Eurasian, she speaks both English and Cantonese fluently. With an IELTS score of 9, she shares her insights into the learning and practice of spoken English- an area where she feels Chinese students of English struggle the most.

Belinda is married with four sons, all of whom are working or studying in London, where she resides with her husband. She spends her leisure time painting and volunteering in her local church.

Belinda Ginns，教育學士，TOSEL，在香港擁有 20 多年的英語講師經驗。她曾於香港不同企業、學校、職業培訓中心及專上院校（包括城市大學及科技大學）任教。她也參與國泰航空人員發展領域的翻譯和溝通促進工作。身為歐亞混血兒，她能說流利的英語和廣東話。因為她 IELTS 考了 9 分，她可以分享她對英文口語學習和練習的見解 - 她認為在香港或其他以華人/亞洲人為主的地方，學生學習和練習英文口語的機會比較少，他們應該提升英文口語的能力，並學習說自然的英語。

Belinda 已婚，有四個兒子。她和丈夫住在倫敦。她利用閒暇時間繪畫並在當地教會做義工。

Discover more about her journey, passions, and creations at:
http://belindaedencreations.com/

User's Guide 使用者指南

Abbreviations 簡寫

sth	something
sb	somebody
sw	somewhere
v	verb
n	noun
adv	adverb
phr v	phrasal verb
v phr	verb phrase
adj phr	adjective phrase
e.g.	for example
US	for US usage
Q tag	question tag
Q	question

Degrees of rudeness 粗俗程度

Mildly rude   -   just slightly 少少俗

Rude   -   rude 粗俗

Vulgar *wallgar*   -   very rude 超俗 / 很粗俗

Introduction 介紹

Why write a book on 'Real English'?

為什麼要寫一本關於「真英文」的書?

We're living in a global era where people are increasingly connected with each other via social media like Facebook, email and other forms of messaging. Ideas are exchanged faster than ever before. People all over the world are communicating a lot more. The vehicle for such transfer of ideas and interaction is language. This language is English. There has never been a greater need to speak and write good English than now, as English is the global language, the lingua franca, the common language that we use to interact with other people universally.

我們生活在一個全球化時代,人們通過 Facebook、電子郵件和其他形式的消息傳遞等社交媒體,越來越多地相互聯繫。思想交流的速度比以往任何時候都快。世界各地的人們都在進行更多的交流。這種思想傳遞和互動的載體是語言。這種語言是英語。從來沒有像現在這樣需要說和寫好的英語,因為英語是全球語言,通用語,是我們用來與他人互動的共同語言。

English is a very important language. Many Hong Kong and Mainland Chinese university students do exchange programmes in Western countries such as Canada, Australia or the US, and many Chinese parents send their children to the UK for education. Why? The reason is clear: they believe that a Western education will give them a better change in life in the future. Moreover, they want to be able to speak good English when they or the children come back to Hong Kong and

China, so they can be head and shoulders above their peers, and hopefully find a good job more easily.

Some parents will even get their toddlers ahead by speaking to them in English themselves, although both parents are Chinese, or by enrolling them in expensive international schools so they get to talk to their Western teachers and friends in English. Mastering written and spoken English is certainly an asset for anyone who wants to progress in life. I, for one, have never had any problem finding a job that I wanted in Hong Kong, because I speak and write good English. My English was always better than the interviewers who interviewed me. With equal qualifications, given the choice between employing someone who speaks good English, and one who doesn't, who would you choose?

英語是一種非常重要的語言。許多香港和中國內地的大學生在加拿大、澳大利亞或美國等西方國家進行交流專案，許多中國父母將孩子送到英國接受教育。為什麼？原因很明顯：他們相信西方教育會給他們未來的生活帶來更好的改變。此外，他們希望當他們或孩子回到香港和中國時能夠說一口流利的英語，這樣他們就可以比同齡人高出一籌，並希望更容易找到一份好工作。一些父母甚至會通過自己用英語與他們交談來讓他們的孩子領先，儘管父母都是中國人，或者讓他們進入昂貴的國際學校，這樣他們就可以用英語與西方老師和朋友交談。掌握英語書面和口語對於任何想要在生活中取得進步的人來說無疑是一筆財富。例如，我在香港從來沒有遇到任何問題找工作，因為我的英語說和寫得很好。我的英語總是比面試我的面試官好。在同等資格的情況下，如果在僱用英語說得很好的人和不會說英語的人之間進行選擇，你會選擇誰？

English is also essential for social harmony. For those who are fortunate enough to go abroad for further education, or those who have migrated to Western countries, one of the things they find they need is acceptance. We want to be accepted in our own culture for sure, but for the duration of the time we're aboard, we also want to be accepted by our Western friends as 'one of them'. Unfortunately, sometimes we Asians face racial discrimination and very often, I find the logic behind this is a linguistic one: They don't speak like us; therefore they aren't one of us. If they're not one of us, they must not like us. If they don't like us, we don't like them! (Crystal, 2010) Discrimination alienates people and creates loneliness, mistrust and resentment. Understanding linguistic barriers is a vital step forward in creating a world with tolerance and respect. It is my hope that students of English in China and Hong Kong can speak English as native speakers do, and thus help tear down such barriers. Sure, we have to master English grammar, but once that's learnt, the next step is to master spoken English.

英語對於社會和諧也是必不可少的。對於那些有幸出國深造的人，或者那些移民到西方國家的人來說，他們發現他們需要的一件事就是接受。我們也希望被我們的西方朋友接受為"他們中的一員"。不幸的是，有時我們亞洲人面臨種族歧視，我經常發現這背後的邏輯是語言上的：他們說話不像我們；因此他們不是我們中的一員。如果他們不是我們中的一員，他們一定不喜歡我們。如果他們不喜歡我們，我們就不喜歡他們！（水晶，2010）歧視疏遠人們，造成孤獨、不信任和怨恨。瞭解語言障礙是創造一個寬容和尊重的世界的重要一步。我希望中國大陸和香港的英語學生能夠像母語人士一樣說英語，從而說明消除這些障礙。當然，我們必須掌握英語語法，但一旦學會了，下一步就是掌握英語口語。

Having good English speakers in business or government positions is important for the image of China and Hong Kong in the eyes of the world. Very often, when I turn on the radio, or hear some government person being interviewed on TV, I invariably hear Hong Kong English – in a distinct Hong Kong tone. Not only is the grammar sometimes wrong, but the words they use are unsuitable in speech, and their tone and/or accent are unnatural. How good would it be for Hong Kong if some of our youngsters have learnt to speak good natural English and have made it to serve in our government! How proud we'd be as Hong Kong people if we speak as good English as some people who live in competing successful economies in Asia!

在商業或政府職位上擁有良好的英語人士對於中國和香港在世界眼中的形象非常重要。很多時候，當我打開收音機，或者聽到一些政府人士在電視上接受採訪時，我總是聽到香港英語 - 以一種獨特的香港語氣。不僅語法有時是錯誤的，他們使用的單詞不適合，他們的語氣和/或口音是不自然的。如果我們的一些年輕人學會了說一口流利的自然英語，和為我們的政府服務，對香港有多好！作為香港人，如果我們能說出像亞洲一些生活在競爭激烈的成功經濟體中的人一樣流利的英語，那將是多麼自豪啊！

However, in my years of teaching English, I have been surprised at how difficult it is for Hong Kong students to speak English even if they have passed their English exams with credits and are studying at well-known universities. Written English has never been a big problem – it can be learnt through books, writing exercises, essays, term papers or exam practice. Spoken English seems to be the area that most students struggle in, and understandably so because we live in Hong Kong, in Asia, and there's little chance to learn the spoken phrases and practice using them with other people in our everyday lives. Therefore, students are not confident in speaking English and they do not want to embarrass themselves by trying, so they never improve.

然而，在我多年的英語教學生涯中，我驚訝地發現，即使香港學生以學分通過了英語考試，並在知名大學學習，說英語是多麼困難。書面英語從來都不是一個大問題 - 它可以通過書籍、寫作練習、論文、學期論文或考試來學習。英語口語似乎是大多數學生掙扎的地方。這是可以理解的，因為我們住在亞洲的香港，幾乎沒有機會學習口語，短語，並在日常生活中與他人練習使用它們。因此，學生對說英語沒有信心，他們不想通過嘗試讓自己難堪，所以他們永遠不會進步。

In a survey done in 2010, when I started working at one of the top universities in Hong Kong, to find out which areas in English the undergraduates wanted help with, I fully expected it to be lectures on how to write term papers, or reports and so on. To my surprise, 80 percent of the students wanted to learn social English. They said they simply did not know how to converse with Westerners: they didn't know the topics, they didn't know how to speak fluently, they didn't know the right words to use in different settings, and they didn't know the right tones or stress for the words. Many of them said they were shy and lacked confidence. I then started social English workshops instead, by popular demand. What an eye-opener that had been! And hence the inspiration for this book!

在 2010 年我開始在香港一所頂尖大學工作時進行的一項調查了瞭解學生在哪些方面需要更多幫助。我完全期望他們會選擇如何撰寫論文或報告等。令我驚訝的是，80%的學生想學習社交英語。他們說他們根本不知道如何與西方人交談：他們不知道主題，他們不知道如何流利地說話，他們不知道在不同環境中使用正確的單詞，他們不知道如何說單詞語氣或重音。他們中的許多人說他們很害羞，缺乏信心。然後，我根據大眾的需求，開始了社交英語研討會。真是大開眼界！因此，這本書的靈感就是來自這裡！

This book is designed to help students learn social English. Heidi and I have highlighted some of the common day-to-day expressions we use in 'real' spoken English – English you hear on the streets in any English-speaking country, but particularly in the U.K. They can be phrasal verbs, colloquial English, idioms or even slang, but for the purposes of this book, I call them all 'expressions'. I've translated them into everyday Cantonese (in some cases, written Chinese) so Hong Kong (and other Chinese readers) can relate them to their own dialects, and be able to fully understand and feel the 'naturalness' of the expressions, so the exact 'feelings' from the words or expressions are not lost.

本書旨在幫助學生學習社交英語。Heidi 和我 介紹了我們在「真」英語中一些常見的日常表達方式 - 一些你可以在任何英語國家的街頭聽到，尤其是在英國。它們可以是短語動詞、口語英語、習語甚至俚語，但為簡化說的方法，我稱它們為'表達句子'。我都把它們翻譯成口語化的廣東話（在某些情況下是書面中文），以便香港（和其他中文讀者）可以將它們與他們自己的方言聯繫起來，並能夠充分理解和感受表達的自然性，因此不會丟失單詞或表達中的確切'感覺'。

I hope that students can remember these expressions more easily because they can understand their nuanced subtleties better. As a result, they can use them more readily in conversations with Western people. I've included examples or the social contexts (SC) in which the expressions can be used. In many cases, I've explained other elements in the dialogues, e.g. vocabulary, grammar, other related expressions and their meanings, U.K/US differences or the tone of certain words/emphasis in the sentences. Please note that I've focused on British English as it is the English that I'm more familiar with.

我希望學生能更容易記住這些表達句子，因為他們可以更好地理解它們的細微差別。因此，他們可以在與西方人的對話中更容易地使用它們。我已經包括了可以使用的表達句子範例或社交情境 (SC)。在很多情況下，我解釋了對話中的其他元素，例如 詞彙、文法、其他相關表達、句子及其意義、英國/美國差異或句子中某些單字/強調的語氣。請注意，我專注於英式英語，因為它是我更熟悉的。

Surely there are hundreds of words and expressions we could learn. But we need to start somewhere. I chose these 120 expressions - 20 more from my last book, because 1) some of them I simply heard people use or I myself have used them over the course of planning this book, and 2) some of them are common words and expressions, so they tend to come up a lot in daily conversations. It is my view that it's not so much the quantity of the words you know, but the ability to use the ones that you've learnt. A huge number of words is confusing and daunting - therefore, a phrase book is not very helpful. I've also not seen anyone holding a phrase book or an encyclopaedia in their hands while conversing with Western people! This book is also unique because in reading the dialogues between A and B, you'll actually learn more than 120 expressions, as they are natural dialogues and therefore will have more idioms or naturally spoken words in them already. Real English is just like that.

當然，我們可以學習數百個單字和表達句子。但我們需要從某個地方開始。我之所以選擇這 120 個字或表達句子（比我上一本書多了 20 個字），是因為 1）其中一些在計劃本書的過程中聽到人們使用或者我自己也使用過。2) 還有一些是常用詞和表達方式，所以它們往往會在日常對話中出現很多。我認為，重要的不是你知道的單詞的數量，而是你學習並應用到的能力。大量的詞彙並沒有什麼幫助。因此，字典不是很有用。我也沒有見過有人在與西方人交談時手裡拿著字典或百科全書！這本書也很獨特，因為在閱讀 A 和 B 之間的對話時，你實際上會學到多過 120 個表達方式，因為它們是自然對話，因此已經有更多的成語或自然口語包括在內。真英文就是這樣的。

This book is an updated version of my previous book, which was published in 2012 in Hong Kong. In this edition. As I have mentioned, there are further elaborations under some of the words, including relevant words and phrases, grammatical use and intonation. The audio CD has also been taken out as both Heidi and I believe that the scenarios and translations are all relevant and easy to understand for most Hong Kong people.

這本書是 2012 年在香港出版上一本書的更新版本。正如我所提到的，有些單字還有進一步的闡述，包括相關單字和片語、文法用法和語調。在這個版本中，我們認為不需要 CD，因為 Heidi 和我相信場景和翻譯對大多數香港人來說都是相關且容易理解的。

What's Wrong with Our Spoken English?

我們的英語口語有什麼問題？

"In the beginning was the Word…" ~ *The Bible*

"太初有道……"~聖經

No one would dispute that the primary function of any language is communication. We live in societies where there are many individuals and it is virtually impossible to live in a society and talk to no one. Human interactions are what set us apart from animals, after all.

沒有人會質疑語言的主要功能是溝通。我們生活在人群中，幾乎不可能不與人交談。人類的交流使我們於動物不同。

However, the societies we live in, as Chinese, are Chinese communities. We speak Chinese. We read Chinese books and newspapers. Our friends are Chinese. How can we then interact with people from different cultures? - We need to speak a 'lingua franca', a common international language. This language is English.

然而，作為中國人，我們生活的社會是華人社會。我們說中文。我們閱讀華語書籍和報紙。我們的朋友是中國或香港人。那麼我們如何與來自不同文化背景的人交流呢？我們需要說一種「通用語言」，一種共同的國際語言。這種語言是英語。

Most of us have been learning English since kindergarten. For the average university student, that is about 15 years of English learning. We are quite familiar with English grammar as we need to understand it in order to do our homework, write essays, assignments or take our exams. However, what we cannot learn in these 15 years is naturally spoken English - English that the average person on the street in an English-speaking country speaks because we don't live there.

我們大多數人從幼兒園開始學習英語。對於普通大學生來說，這大約是 15 年的英語學習。我們非常熟悉英語語法，因為我們需要理解它才能做家庭作業、寫論文、作業或參加考試。然而，在這 15 年裡，我們無法學到的是自然的英語口語 - 英語國家街上的普通人會說的英語，因為我們不住在那裡。

Moreover, emphasis in the classroom has always been on written English as we need it to pass our English exams or get higher grades in our written assignments. Spoken English gets left behind. No wonder most Hong Kong university students become tongue-tied when they have to converse with a foreigner. No wonder the English standard among our youngsters is dropping. Hong Kong needs to catch up if it wants to maintain a competitive edge against economies like Singapore, where almost everyone can speak fluent English. So what's the problem with our spoken English?

此外，課堂上的重點一直是書面英語，因為我們需要它來通考我們的英語考試或在作業中獲得更高的成績。英語口語就被拋在後面。難怪大多數香港大學生在與外國人交談時會口結舌。難怪我們年輕人的英語水準正在下降。如果香港想要保持與新加坡等經濟體的競爭優勢，就需要迎頭趕上，新加坡幾乎每個人都能說一口流利的英語。那麼我們的英語口語有什麼問題呢？

Problems

問題

1. We don't have enough vocabulary of spoken words.

我們沒有足夠的口語詞彙。

Students of English often learn complicated written English words at schools or universities. We've been told that a longer word is better than a simple one. We've been taught to use 'academic words' in our essays. While this may be correct in academic work (and I say 'may' because one of the rules of good writing is not to use a longer word when a shorter, simpler word will do), it's inappropriate for oral communication. We need to learn different vocabulary or phrases for this purpose, and hence the importance of this book!

英語學生經常在學校或大學學習複雜的書面英語單詞。我老師總是說較長的單詞比簡單的單詞更好。我們被教導在論文中使用「學術詞彙」。雖然這在學術工作中可能是正確的（我說 '可能' 是因為良好寫作的規則之一是不使用較長的單詞，而較短，更簡單的單詞就可以了），但它不適合口頭溝通。為此，我們需要學習不同的詞彙或短語，這就是為什麼這本書如此重要！

2. We transfer written words to our spoken vocabulary.

我們將書面文字轉移到我們的口語詞彙中。

Another problem is that there are many different ways in English to say the same things, but students tend to prefer using long difficult words to express their meaning. E.g. 'desire to' etc. The choice of the word is dependent on the occasion/situation in which the word is used. You wouldn't wear a formal dinner jacket to a beach party. It's the same with the use of formal words in informal settings. E.g. 'wish to' is more appropriate in a letter. "I wish to have an opportunity to discuss this with you further", whereas 'want' is more suitable in a spoken conversation: "I want to talk about this with you a bit more". Both carry the same meaning, but the words used in spoken English are a lot simpler. The problem is students of English often think that written formal words are better. They try to 'show off' their vocabulary. Please see my next section on 'Bookish English' for more explanation on this point.

另一個問題是，英語中有很多不同的方式來表達同樣的事情，但學生傾向於使用長而困難的單詞來表達它們的含義。例如 '渴望' 等。該詞的選擇取決於使用該詞的場合/情況。你不會穿正式的晚餐夾克去參加海灘派對。在非正式場合使用正式詞語也是如此。例如，'希望' 在一封信中更合適。「我希望有機會與你進一步討論這個問題」，而「想要更適合在口頭對話中」，我想和你多談談這個問題"。兩者都具有相同的含義，但英語口語中使用的單詞要簡單得多。問題是英語學生經常認為書面形式單詞更好。他們試圖炫耀他們的詞彙量。請參閱我的下一節 'Bookish English'，以獲取有關這一點的更多解釋。

Many English words can be both written and spoken but there are also many words that are only spoken and not written, simply because it would not be polite to write them down in documents. These spoken words are casual in nature. Many of them are even rude or offensive because they carry a lot of emotions in them and they act as a way for speakers to release their tension. Slang words are an example of words in this category. Some of these words are included in this book. Readers need to be careful when using them as they can come across as rude. The degree of offensiveness is indicated in the book with these words, so readers can understand them better.

許多英語單詞可以寫和說，但也有很多單詞只是口語和不是書面，僅僅是因為它們寫在文檔中是不禮貌的。這些口語本質上是隨意的。他們中的許多人甚至是粗魯或冒犯的，因為這些字是情感的字，講者用這些字來表達他們的心情。俚語是此類別中單詞的一個例子。其中一些詞包含在本書中。讀者在使用它們時需要小心，因為它們可能被認為是粗魯的。這些字在書中已標示了粗魯的程度，讓讀者更能理解。

Slang or colloquial English sometimes does not follow grammatical rules because the aim is to convey a message quickly and to the point, and sometimes being too busy with grammar when we speak can cause English to sound stilted and unnatural. E.g. 'innit?' is the spoken form of the question tag 'isn't it?' that tags onto questions like "it's great, isn't it?" Basic grammar says question tags change according to the verb in the question part of the sentence e.g. "It's raining, isn't it?" and "They're crazy, aren't they?" However, young people in some parts of London nowadays use 'innit?' as an unchanging tag, so they say "They're crazy, innit?" This tag is by no means correct grammatically, (and I don't encourage anyone to use it) but 'innit' as an unchanging tag might become more common as time goes on. But for now, 'innit' is only spoken and is used in questions like this: "It's interesting, innit?" (Davidson, Planet Word: Penguin Books 2011)

俚語或口語英語有時不遵循語法規則，因為目的是快速而充滿情感地傳達訊息。有時當我們說話時忙於語法會導致英語聽起來生硬和不自然。例如，'innit' 是問題標籤「不是嗎？」的口語形式，它標記在諸如「這很棒，不是嗎？」之類的問題上。基本語法說問題標籤根據句子問題部分中的動詞而變化，例如「下雨了，不是嗎？」「他們瘋了，不是嗎？」然而，現在倫敦某些地區的年輕人使用 'innit' 作為不變的標籤，所以他們說「他們瘋了，innit？」。這個標籤在語法上絕不是正確的（我不鼓勵任何人使用它），但隨著時間的推移，'innit' 作為一個不變的標籤可能會變得更加普遍。但就目前而言，'innit' 只被說出來，並用於這樣的問題：「這很有趣，innit?」（大衛森，星球之詞：企鵝圖書 2011）

3. Learners of English in Asia do not have enough chance to practise what they know or have learnt about spoken English.

亞洲的英語學習者沒有足夠的機會練習他們所知道或學到的英語口語。

In Hong Kong, people live in a majority Chinese environment. Cantonese is spoken there. Most people who live in Hong Kong or China are Chinese. They don't always have Western friends to practice English with. I've always found it surprising when I was teaching in universities in Hong Kong, that how few students actually had Western friends because in general, students are too scared or shy, or perhaps just "can't be bothered" to make an effort to converse with people who speak a different language from them. The fewer Western friends they have, the less the chance there is for them to practice speaking English. The less practice they get, the harder it is when they have to do it, and so the vicious cycle goes on. The thing with a language is this: if you don't use it, you'll lose it. The more you use it, the better it gets. Speaking gets easier and easier with practice until one day, we don't even have to think too much about it - it just comes. Practice is the key.

在香港，人們生活在以華人為主的環境中。那裡使用的語言是廣東話。住在那裡的大多數人都是香港中國人。他們並不 沒有西方朋友一起練習英語。我總是覺得在香港大學教學中感到驚訝的是，很少學生真正認識西方朋友，因為一般來說，學生太害怕或害羞，或者可能只是懶得努力與說不同語言的人交談。

他們擁有的西方朋友越少，他們練習說英語的機會就越少。他們練習得越少，他們必須這樣做的時候就越難，所以惡性循環還在繼續。語言的問題是：如果你不使用它，你就會失去它。你使用它的次數越多，你就會說得更好。隨著練習，說話變得越來越容易，直到有一天，我們甚至不必考慮太多 - 就可以做到。練習是關鍵。

4. Students lack confidence when they finally get a chance to converse in English.

當學生終於有機會用英語交談時，他們缺乏信心。

They try to find the right words, and they stutter, then they try to say something but unfortunately the wrong things - in the wrong tone or pronunciation, or both. Our Western friends will either find it quite funny and carry on with the friendship, or they might not want to continue making friends with people who don't speak like them, pretty much the same reason as Chinese people not wanting to make an effort to mix with western people (pt 3 above). The less they mix, the less confident they become. Confidence is a real issue for a lot of Hong Kong students.

他們試圖找到正確的單詞，他們口窒窒，然後他們試圖說些什麼，但不幸說錯了 - 錯誤的語氣或發音，或兩者兼而有之。我們的西方朋友有些覺得這很有趣並繼續保持友誼，但有些可能不想繼續與那些說話不像他們的人交朋友，這與中國人不想努力與西方人混在一起的原因幾乎相同（上文第 3 點）。他們混得越少，他們就越不自信。對於許多香港學生來說，信心是一個很大的問題。

5. Students of English do not immerse themselves in English.

英語學生不會沉浸在英語中。

Not only are most people happy to just make friends with people in their own circles, people are also too lazy to listen to English songs, watch English movies without subtitles, or read English magazines or newspapers. A sure way to learn a language, whether spoken or written, is to immerse yourself into that culture- to learn what that culture is about, and to try to learn its language from different angles- from songs, poetry, movies, media and of course books. The digital age is really useful for learning English - for you can easily log onto YouTube and hear people from all over the world speak natural, spoken English. We can also surf online in English. There's so much to learn and so much of it can be learnt online! How much easier does it get?

不僅大多數人樂於與自己圈子裡的人交朋友，人們也懶得聽英文歌曲，看沒有字幕的英文電影，或者看英文雜誌或報紙。學習一種語言的一個可靠方法，無論是口語還是書面語言，都是讓自己沉浸在那個國家的文化中，瞭解這種文化是怎樣的，並嘗試從不同的角度學習它的語言 - 從歌曲、詩歌、電影、媒體，當然還有書籍。數字時代對於學習英語非常有用 - 因為您可以輕鬆上 YouTube 並聽到來自世界各地的人們說自然的英語口語。我們也可以用英語在上網。很多東西可以在網上學習！多麼容易啊！

Chinglish

中文和英文混合

We don't want to sound 'Chinglish' (Chinese and English mixed together) when we speak English, and we don't want to sound 'bookish' either. Bookish English is when educated people like legislators, and university professors speak 'literal,' or else I call it 'Bookish English' - correct of course, but formal - unsuitable for day-to-day English, and therefore not 'natural' sounding. The spoken flavour is lost, as words are more suitable for formal scripts, or for their jobs; between people who understand those words and speak the same way. Both Chinglish and Bookish English hinder Chinese people from speaking real English. A section on bookish English can be found in this book.

當我們說英語時，我們不想聽起來像 'Chinglish'（中文和英文混合在一起），我們也不想聽起來 'bookish'（書卷氣）。書本英語是指受過教育的人，如立法者、大學教授說 '字面意思的英語'。我稱之為 '書本' 英語 - 當然是正確的，但很傳統 - 不適合日常英語，因此聽起來不自然。口語的味道消失了，因為單詞更適合傳統正式的信息，或者適合在工作中使用；或和同樣方式說話的人溝通。中文英語和書本英語都阻礙中國人說真正的英語。你可以在本書中找到一些關於書卷英文的資料。

One needs real or almost real situations, and the environment in which to practice speaking a language. Therefore, the social contexts (SCs) in this book were thought out with careful consideration for their appropriateness within the Hong Kong setting. The dialogues in the examples were written to be as close to what you would hear in real life as possible. The key to this is to imagine the situation, learn the expression, and imagine yourself using it in similar situations in your own life, in Hong Kong or abroad. Imagination is an important part as the expression will go deeper into your subconscious. Next time when a similar setting or situation arises, you'd be more likely to think of the appropriate word/expression. With time and constant practice, you'll find yourself speaking, like a native speaker does - not struggling at all!

我們需要真實或相近真實的情況，以及練習說語言的環境。因此，我們已仔細考慮了本書中的社交情境 (SC) - 它們在香港環境中的適當性。示例中的對話盡可能接近您在現實生活中聽到的內容。這裡的關鍵是學習表達方式的想像力，並想像自己在香港或海外的生活中的類似情況下使用它。想像力是一個重要的部分，因為這些字會更深入你的潛意識。下次你在類似的情境時，您更有可能想到合適的單詞/表達方式。隨著時間和不斷的練習，你會發現自己說話就像母語人士一樣 - 一點也不難！

Bookish English

書本英語

"He that will write well in any tongue, must follow this counsel of Aristotle, to speak as the common people do, to think as wise men do; and so should every man understand him, and the judgment of wise men allow him." - Roger Adcham.

"能用任何語言寫得很好的人，必須遵循亞里士多德的忠告，像普通人一樣說話，像智者一樣思考；每個人都應該理解他，智者的判斷允許他" - 羅傑·阿德查姆。

In 1977, New York state was the first state in America to set up a "General-Purpose Plain English Law" that stated that business language should be for the consumers and not commercial transactions (Steinberg: Plain English, 1977). This was a move towards a nontechnical vocabulary; a clear and succinct usage, using words with common and everyday meaning.

1977年，紐約州是美國第一個建立「通用簡單英語法」的州，該法律規定商業語言應該面向消費者，而不是商業交易（Steinberg：Plain English，1977）。這是向非技術詞彙的轉變；清晰簡潔的用法，使用具有常見和日常含義的單詞。

In fact this move to the use of 'plain English' started much earlier in the U.K. In 1948 Sir Ernest Gowers, a civil servant of the British Government, was asked to compile a manual which would help the government officials to avoid using overly complicated words in writing, and to use more clear and simple words. Written communication had become almost incomprehensible with terminologies that corporations and government offices would use, but not anybody else. A lot of those words were, and still are, what Gowers called 'overworked' words: e.g. utilize instead of use, envisage instead of imagine, visualize instead of see (Davidson, Planet Word, 2011).

事實上，這種使用「普通英語」的舉動在英國很早就開始了。1948年，英國政府的公務員歐內斯特·高爾斯爵士（Sir Ernest Gowers）被要求編寫一本手冊，說明政府官員避免在書面上使用過於複雜的詞語，並使用更清晰和簡單的詞語。書面交流幾乎無法理解公司和政府部門會使用的術語，但其他任何人都不會。其中很多詞過去是，現在仍然是，高爾斯所說的'過度勞累'詞：例如利用而不是使用，設想而不是想像，想像而不是看到（戴維森，星球詞，2011）。

George Orwell (1930-50) in 'Politics and English Language' (cited in Crystal: The Cambridge Encyclopaedia of Language, 2010) set out six rules for elementary English usage, and one of those rules was 'Never use a long word when a short one will do'. In 'The Elements of Style' 2005, Strunk warns against using 'fancy words'. He said "Do not be tempted by a twenty-dollar word when there is a ten-center handy, ready and able". He recommends using Anglo-Saxon words, words that are simple and have clear-cut meanings, in preference to Latin words, words that are more elaborate. If this is so for writing, it is even more important for speaking.

喬治·奧威爾（George Orwell，1930-50）在《政治與英語》（Politics and English Language）一書中（引自《水晶：劍橋語言百科全書》，2010 年）列出了初級英語使用的六條規則，其中一條規則是「永遠不要使用長詞，而短詞就可以了」。在 2005 年的「風格元素」中，Strunk 警告不要使用「花哨的詞」。他說：「當有一個十個中心方便，準備好和有能力時，不要被一個二十美元的單詞所誘惑」。他建議使用盎格魯-撒克遜語單詞，這些單詞簡單且具有明確的含義，而不是拉丁單詞，即更精緻的單詞。如果寫作是這樣，那麼說話就更重要了。

Compare:

比較：

Refuse and rubbish shall not be collected from the site or receptacles thereon before the hour of 8:00 am or after the hour of 6:00 pm every day.

「不得在每天上午 8：00 之前或下午 6：00 之後從這個位置或其容器中收集廢物和垃圾」。

And: *"We will collect your garbage between 8:00 am and 6:00 pm every day."*

並且：「我們每天將在上午 8：00 至下午 6：00 之間收集您的垃圾」。

(Keith Allan and Kate Burridge, Forbidden Words: Taboo and the Censoring of Language, 2006)

(Keith Allan 和 Kate Burridge，禁忌詞：禁忌和語言審查，2006)

"We are considering purchasing this residence."

「我們正在考慮購買這套住宅。」

And: *"We are thinking about buying this house."*

並且：「我們正在考慮購買這所房子。」

"Don't forget to request for assistance."

「不要忘記要求協助。」

And: *"Don't forget to ask for help."*

並且：「不要忘記尋求幫助。」

In all the three examples above, the second lines are much clearer in meaning than the first.

在上面的所有三個例子中，第二行的含義比第一行清晰得多。

Overly formal words confuse meaning and are unsuitable for everyday oral communication. It's tempting to show off your vocabulary by using a harder, multi-syllable word rather than a simple mono-syllable word but it's actually more appropriate to use simpler words in daily speech.

過於正式的詞語會混淆含義，不適合日常口頭交流。通過使用更難的多音節單詞而不是簡單的單音節單詞來炫耀您的詞彙量是很誘人的，但實際上在日常講話中使用更簡單的單詞更合適。

****

I had a very interesting experience which demonstrates my point effectively. One day my 8-year-old son was sick. I took him to see a doctor. The doctor was Chinese, and my son cannot speak Cantonese so the doctor had to ask him questions in English.

我有一個非常有趣的經歷，有效地證明瞭我的觀點。有一天，我 8 歲的兒子生病了。我帶他去看醫生。醫生是中國人，我兒子不會說廣東話，所以醫生不得不用英語問他問題。

This is how the conversation went:

談話是這樣的：

Doctor: *What are your complaints?*

醫生：你有什麼抱怨？

Son: huh?

兒子：嗯？

Me: He asked you what's wrong with you.

我：他問你怎麼了。

Son: Shoulder and tummy pains

兒子：肩膀和肚子痛

Doctor: *Regarding your shoulder pain - what is your sensation when it occurs?*

醫生：關於你的肩膀疼痛 - 當它發生時你有什麼感覺？

Son: huh??

兒子：嗯？？

Me: He asked you how it feels when it happens.

我：他問你當它發生時是什麼感覺。

Son: painful

兒子：痛

Doctor: *Have you had any injuries?*

醫生：你受傷了嗎？

Son: huh??

兒子：嗯？？

Me: He asked you if you've hurt yourself.

我：他問你有沒有跌倒。

Son: No

兒子：沒有

Doctor: *Does the pain subside if you extend your arms?*

醫生：如果你伸出手臂，疼痛會消退嗎？

Son: huh???

兒子：嗯？？

Me: He asked you if the pain goes away if you stretch out your arms.

我：他問你，如果你伸出雙臂，疼痛會不會消失。

Son: No

兒子：不會

Doctor: *Regarding your stomach pain - where is the location of your pain?*

醫生：關於你的胃痛 - 你的疼痛在哪裡？

Son: huh??

兒子：嗯？？

Me: He asked you where it hurts.

我：他問你哪裡疼。

Son: Here (pointing)

兒子：這裡（指點）

Doctor: *This is your bowels, not your gastronomic tract.*

醫生：這是你的腸子，不是你的食道。

Son: What???

兒子：什麼？？？

The conversation went on like this for 10 minutes!! Totally true story. It ended with *"I'll prescribe you medication sufficient for 3 days"*, instead of "I'll give you medicine for 3 days". My poor son!

談話就這樣持續了 10 分鐘！！完全真實的故事。它以「我會給你開足夠 3 天的藥」結束，而不是「我會給你 3 天的藥」。我可憐的兒子！

He is a child - fair enough - but if we can make sure an 8-year-old understands what we're saying, we're doing well. Long words do not convey the best meaning in oral English. They make meaning difficult to understand!

他是個孩子 - 可理解的 - 但如果我們可以確保一個 8 歲的孩子理解我們在說什麼，我們就做得很好了。長詞不能傳達英語口語的最佳含義。它們使含義難以理解！

Apart from making grammatical mistakes, most educated Hong Kong people speak like this:

除了犯語法錯誤外，大多數受過教育的香港人都是這樣說的：

Legislator: "*We're seeing some increase in…..and a decrease in…*" instead of: "We're seeing a rise in… and a drop in…." or "…has gone up, but….has gone down"

立法者：「我們看到 (some increase in) 一些增加……和 (a decrease in) 減少」…而不是：「我們看到..有上升，還有下降...」或…「上升了，但是……下降了」

Professor: "*…get a satisfactory performance.*" Why not say… "do well"? "*…the…maintained due to the…*" Why not say… "the…continues because…"?

教授：「。。。獲得滿意的表現。」 為什麼不說...「做得好」？「...這。。維持由於...」 為什麼不說...「這...繼續因為...」？

Social Workers: "...*to enhance social services*". 'Enhance' is a favourite word because it sounds academic. Why not say to "improve social services"?

社會工作者:「...增強社會服務」。人們喜歡使用「增強」(enhance) 這個字,因為聽起來很學術。為什麼不說「改善社會服務"?

The more educated the person, the higher the chance the person will have this problem.

受教育程度越高的人,遇到這個問題的機會就越大。

English Native speakers

英語為母語的人

Compare the above phrases with some things I've heard native speakers say. Note the simple, informal words, the idioms and the metaphor:

將上述短語與比較我聽英語為母語的人士的說法比較。注意簡單的非正式詞,習語和隱喻:

"...*this leads up to*..."/ "*it's down to*..." (phrasal verbs)/ "....*because of*..." (informal words)/ "*this has a lot of to do with*..." (simple words)/ "*put a positive spin on* (idiom)/ "...*put a gun to your head*" (= force you - metaphor)

「...這導致...」/「它歸結為...」(短語動詞)/「因為...」(非正式字的字)/「這與...有關係」(簡單的字)/「給...一個積極

xxxi

的旋轉」(a positive spin) (成語)...用槍指著你的頭 (put a gun to your head) (=強迫你 - 隱喻)

Read the following conversation by two English native speakers.

閱讀以下兩位以英語為母語的人的對話。

Two people talking in a work canteen:

兩個人在工作食堂聊天：

A: Hey, do you know this new person who *came to* (simple word- not 'joined our workforce') work this week? - Kathy, her name is. I found out that she's extremely *switched on* (phrasal verb = know a lot of things)!

A: 嘿，你知道這個新人本周來（簡單的字 -「不是沒有加入我們的工作團隊」）工作嗎？- 她的名字是凱西。我發現她非常聰明（ switched on - 短語動詞 = 知道很多事情）！

B: Now what have you heard?

B: 你聽到了什麼？

A: It's *hard work listening* (simple phrase: hard work + ing) to her - she talks *nineteen to the dozen* (a lot)! I had to *put up with* (phrasal verb = let sb do/say sth even though it's difficult for you) her for half an hour, but according to Kathy, and she does seem to have *friends in high places* = friends who are important): we're going to have a good raise this year!

A: 聽她說話很辛苦（簡單的短語：hard work +ing）— 她說十九對十幾個 (nineteen to the dozen=很多）！我要忍受她半小時（短

語動詞=讓 sb 做/說 sth，即使這對你來說很難），但根據凱西，她似乎有高位的朋友(friends in high places =重要的朋友)：我們今年會有一個很好的加薪！

B: Really? I'd *take that with a pinch of salt* (idiom = don't believe much of it)!

B: 真？我會加一點鹽（成語=不太相信）！

A: Well, that's what I thought, so I went to the boss and got it *straight from the horse's mouth* (metaphor and idiom = get confirmation from sb)! *M's the word* (informal expression = keep quiet. M refers to the sound the mouth makes when it's closed) - ok? It's not official yet.

A: 嗯，我就是這麼想的，所以我去找老闆，直接從馬的嘴裏得到消息，（比喻和成語=得到 sb 的確認）！M 是這個字（非正式字 =保持沉默, 不要告訴任何人。M 是指嘴閉合時發出的聲音）- ok？這還不是官方的消息。

This is not an uncommon conversation between two native speakers. Note the conversation is dotted with idioms, metaphors, phrasal verbs, simple words and expressions.

這是兩個母語人士之間的對話並不少見。請注意，對話中點綴著成語、隱喻、短語動詞、簡單的單字和表達方式。

It is our hope that this book will be accessible and useful to all Chinese learners of English, most particularly the Hong Kong Chinese communities who have recently moved over to the U.K. Starting a new home in a strange environment is not easy, as it's been my experience in different parts of the world, but we believe that this book will help many to integrate into British society. If we try to speak like the locals do when we develop new relationships, distance is drawn closer, and the integration process will be doubly fast and effective.

我們希望所有香港及中國英語學習者，尤其是最近移居英國的香港人，都能讀懂本書並受益。在一個陌生的環境中開始新家並不容易 - 我也曾在很多國家生活過，知道適應是很困難的。但我們相信這本書將幫助許多香港人融入英國社會。 如果我們在發展新關係時盡量用當地人的方式說話，距離就會拉近，融入就會加倍快速和有效。

So, let's get started!

讓我們開始吧！

Preface 前言

This book aims to give students a list of everyday words, phrases, and expressions that they can use in everyday situations. It's a very practical book and there are lots of social situations (social contexts [SC]) to bring the expressions alive. I had them translated into everyday Cantonese (and written Chinese in some cases), so students can get a flavour of what the expressions really mean - in their own language so they can remember more easily, and so hopefully use them more readily.

本書旨在為學生提供可以在日常情況下使用的日常口頭短語，或單詞。這是一本非常實用的書，有很多社會情境（SC）可以使表達生動起來。我已將其翻譯成日常廣東話 (在某些情況下還有書面中文），因此學生可以用自己的語言瞭解該表達的真正含義，這樣他們就可以更容易地記住它們，因此希望更容易地使用它們。

I know there are a number of books in the bookstores on spoken English, written and translated by Chinese people. However, very often these books are written with no or little background knowledge of British cultural norms. The expressions the authors choose, the examples they use and the corresponding translations are also unsuitable for Hong Kong people in the U.K. If learners can't relate to the examples and the translations in a book, they will never remember the words and phrases, let alone use them.

我知道書店裡有很多由中國人寫和翻譯的英文口語書。然而，所選的詞語與日常生活無關。他們也不了解英國人的生活方式。

他們使用的例子和相應的翻譯都不適合香港人在英國使用。如果學習者無法完全理解字的含意，他們將無法說正確的英語。

Being both English and Chinese, and having grown up in Hong Kong, and having taught English for many years in Hong Kong, I understand fully the problems faced by Chinese students learning English, the social situations they might encounter when abroad, their mind set and the responses they might have. 'Real English' is written with such insider's knowledge. I feel that 'Real English' is going to be a very useful book for those who want to speak English naturally, as native speakers do.

我在香港長大，並是混血兒，也在香港教英文多年，我完全理解中國學生學習英語的問題，他們在外國可能面臨的社交場合，他們的心態和反應。《真英文》就是用這些內幕的知識寫的。我覺得《真英文》對於那些想像母語人士一樣自然地說英語的人來說將會是一本非常有用的書。

I would like to thank my family, especially my husband James for supporting me through the writing journey. Many thanks also to Heidi Leung for her superb and lively Cantonese translation.

我要感謝我的家人，尤其是我的丈夫 James 在寫作過程中對我的支持。也非常感謝為本書的內容做出貢獻的 Heidi Leung，感謝她精湛而生動的廣東話翻譯。

Thank you also, my readers, for buying this book. The fact that you have bought the book probably means you want to work on the area of spoken English. I encourage you to go through the expressions one by one, imagining each scenario, then imagine yourself in a similar situation in Hong Kong, your own country or abroad, or in the U.K. You will begin to understand the correct situations in which to use these words. Once you understand their usage, you can then remember them more easily and be able to use them more readily.

也感謝你們，我的讀者。你買了這本書可能是你想提升你的英文口語。我鼓勵你閱讀這些字，句子和例子，想像每個場景，然後想像自己在香港、在你自己的國家、外國，特別是在英國類似的情況。您將開始理解如何正確使用這些單字或句子。

Contents

Dedication — i

About the Author — ii

User's Guide 使用者指南 — iv

Introduction 介紹 — v

Preface 前言 — xxxv

Contents — xxxviii

Chapter 1 Everyday words and expressions — 1

1. A bit much – a bit unreasonable - 有啲過份/有些過份 — 1

2. Been there, done that – done sth before, experienced it before - 做過啦 — 3

3. Bloke/ chap / guy – (US) (n) – a man – 男人 — 5

4. Have a chat – talk about something casually - 傾下計/ 聊天 — 6

5. Cheers – thank you – 唔該/ 謝謝 — 7

6. Chuck it / bin it / ditch it – (v) – to throw something away, to forget about it - 唔要，擱置/ 不要，擱置 — 9

7. Comfy – (adj) – comfortable - 舒服 — 10

8. Dodgy – (adj) – very doubtful, suspicious - 好狡猾，懷疑，有啲問題/ 有些問題 — 12

9. Fags (n); Booze (n) – cigarettes - 煙仔 / 香煙; alcohol - 酒 — 13

10. Fancy doing something / Fancy something / someone (v) – like to do, like - 想做，鐘意/ 喜歡 — 15

11. Get it – understand – 明白 ，收到 — 17

12. Have a go / It's somebody's go – have a try, sb's turn - 嘗試，到你喇 / 到你了   18

13. (It's a) good job (that)…– lucky – 好在/ 幸好..   19

14. Grab some lunch / snack / have a bite to eat – get sth to eat - 去買啲嘢食 / 去買一些食物   20

15. To be honest / Honestly! (adv) – actually, to tell you the truth, please don't do that! (embarrassing) - 講真吖，唔係咁下話（尷尬）/真心話，不是這樣的嗎？   22

16. Idea / clue (n) – know 知   23

17. Kind of / sort of – quite (transition words) - 幾（過渡詞）/ 有點兒   25

18. Knick (v) – steal 偷   27

19. Leg it (v) – to run, to run away from sth/sb - 閃，閃避/ 走，走避   28

20. Like – transition word when thinking what to say next - 就話，咁，就，諗緊同事（過渡詞）   29

21. Go to the loo / desperate for the loo / desperate for a pee (mildly rude) – go to toilet, want to go to the toilet badly - 去廁所，好想去廁所，好急尿 （少少俗）/撒尿   32

22. No problem / no worries – it's ok - 冇問題/沒有問題   33

23. Pop – go somewhere quickly for a short time (v) - 過一過嚟，入一入嚟/ 過一過來，入一入來   34

24. Quid (n) – sterling pound - 英鎊   36

25. Reckon (v) – think - 諗，覺得   37

26. Let's rock and roll (let's roll)! – eager to start to do sth - 迫不及待想去做   38

27. Sorted / sort something out / get sorted – problem solved, solve the problem, get organized - 搞掂，搞掂一個問題，搞返掂佢/收拾，解決了問題   40

28. That'll do –it's enough - 都夠㗎喇，唔使再做，講/足夠，不用再做，說   42

29. Tricky (adj) – problematic, difficult to do - 難啲㗎/難處理的   43

30. We'll see, won't we (Q tag) – see how the situation develops - 到時咪知囉，睇吓點/看看吧   45

31. Whatever – however sb likes it - 是但啦 / 沒有所謂   46

32. What have you / what not – whatever else, 'etc' - 嗰啲嘢 / 那些東西   47

33. What're you up to? What's up with you? How's it going? (Q) – greeting - 最近點呀？/ 近來怎麼樣啊？   49

34. Swamped (adj) –overwhelmed 冧檔 - 超忙 - 很忙   50

35. A walk in the park -an easy thing to do - 超易, 很容易的   52

36. The real deal - someone or something that is very good and has the qualities that people say they have - 堅嘢，超勁, 真貨，很勁   54

37. Get some air - to go for a walk – 去唞啖氣，出去行一下   55

38. How one's doing for time? - does one have time, is one in a hurry – 你趕唔趕時間, 你趕不趕時間   56

39. What's that all about? – when you don't understand why something is so popular, or the reason why it's there - 搞乜鬼野，搞咩，搞什麼鬼   57

40. Are you up for ___? (Q) - do you want to do this thing? - 你想唔想去做, 你想不想去做   59

Chapter 2 Idioms / phrasal verbs 俗語，成語　　　　　61

41. All over the place / shop – everywhere, disorganized - 亂晒籠 / 一塌糊塗　　　61

42. At the end of the day – when everything else has been taken into consideration - 坐底 始終　　　63

43. Bang on about something (phr v)– to talk a lot about sth in a boring way - 猛咁講（好煩），囉唆 / 講不完（很煩）　　　64

44. Chill out (phr v) – to calm down, relax - 冷靜吖，出去玩吓啦 / 冷靜一下，出去玩一下　　　66

45. A close shave – very close to having an accident - 差啲就賴嘢 / 差一點就出事，很危險　　　67

46. Crack someone up – to make sb laugh a lot - 搞笑 / 令人發大笑　　　68

47. Crack on (phr v) – to continue - 繼續　　　70

48. Crank it up (phr v)– to increase - 加重啲，加大啲 / 加重一些，加大一些　　　72

49. A dead loss – sb / sth useless - 好屎，嘥氣啦 / 沒用的，浪費時間的　　　73

50. Dive in (phr v)– to jump into doing sth eagerly - 好心急咁樣去做啲嘢 / 急不及待　　　74

51. Fair enough – ok, reasonable, understandable - 有道理，係嘅 / 對啊　　　75

52. Fingers crossed – to hope for the best - 希望，希望好運啦　　　78

53. Fire away (U.K.) / Shoot (US) to say - 講呀　　　79

54. Go haywire – out of control - 癲晒，亂晒籠 / 失去控制，混亂　　81

55. Go out with somebody – to have a date with sb, to have a relationship with sb - 拍拖　　82

56. Go with the flow (idiom)– let the event / situation develop naturally - 順其自然　　83

57. A good / bad call – a good/bad decision - 好 / 壞嘅決定，好在，蠢咗 / 好 / 壞的決定，蠢了　　85

58. Have a lot of / no time for something / somebody – like/not like or interested/not interested in sth/sb - 鍾意，唔鍾意, li-ke, 唔 li-ke / 喜歡，不喜歡　　86

59. Have too much on someone's plate (idiom)– too occupied, busy - 太多嘢做 / 太多事情要做　　88

60. It's a long shot – sth that is difficult to do - 都幾難喎　　89

61. Lose the plot (idiom)– cannot understand/deal with what is happening, confused - 唔明白，九唔搭八 / 不明白　　90

62. Mess around / faff / goof / muck around (phr v) – to play around, not serious - 搞搞震，玩玩吓 / 胡鬧　　93

63. Off the top of somebody's head (idiom)– just guessing or using memory, without thinking hard - 就咁諗 / 就這樣想　　95

64. On the trot – one after another, continuously – 連續 / 不停地　　96

65. Pull it off (phr v)– succeed in doing sth difficult - 做得到　　97

66. Put foot in it – to be involved in sth - 干涉，架樑，洗濕咗頭 / 牽涉　　99

67. Ring a bell (idiom)– familiar, to be reminded of - 好熟，有印象 / 熟悉　　101

68. Rip off (phr v) – to get someone to pay more than they need to - 搵笨 / 欺騙　　102

69. Screw something up / mess up / botch up / cock up (phr v) – to do sth badly - 搞禍咗，攪喎晒 / 弄得很差　　104

70. Skive off (phr v)– to avoid doing work - 蛇王，走堂 / 溜走，逃學　　105

71. Suss something / somebody out (phr v)– to find out, understand about sth/sb - 睇穿，發覺，知，明白　　107

72. That's life (idiom)– just the way things are: we have to accept them - 就係咁㗎喇 / 就是如此了　　108

73. Up somebody's street (idiom) – suitable for sb - 啱晒你啦 / 適合　　109

74. On the same page – (idiom) Same understanding on the topic being discussed - 你明白我，我明白你,有共通，大家都清楚明白　　111

75. Cave in (phr v) - to give up – 屈服　　113

76. Have a word with someone - To talk it over with someone – 同佢講吓！- 和他/她說一下吧！　　114

77. Ticking the box - to do what needs to be done because of rules and regulations – 求其寫，交功課（守則，規矩）　　116

78. You can bank on it - you're sure, confident it will happen/won't happen. You can rely on it - 肯定會/唔會發生　　117

79. To have a brainwave –to have a sudden idea of what to do - 突然之間諗到個想法 / 突然知道該怎麼做　　119

80. Keep an eye /ear out for something (idiom) - to pay attention by looking (eye) or listening (ear) - 睇住/聽住, 看著/聽著　　120

Chapter 3 Feelings words and Exclamations   122

81. Cheesed off / hacked off / peeved / bummed – annoyed, disappointed - 激氣，失望 / 生氣   122

82. Chuffed to bits / thrilled to bits – extremely happy - 超開心 / 很開心   124

83. Crap (n) / crappy (adj) sth of poor quality, stupid or bad (mildly rude) - 垃圾，好屎，廢話，廢物（少少俗）很差   125

84. Crummy – bad quality – 勁差 / 品質差   127

85. Daft – silly - 蠢，戇居 / 傻的   128

86. Dicey – dangerous - 危險   130

87. Do somebody's head in – (phr v) – feel confused and annoyed - 搞到頭都暈埋，煩死   131

88. Gutted – extremely sad or disappointed - 非常失望   132

89. Can / can't hack it (v)-can/can't handle it, take it - 忍受得到，唔到 / 忍受不到   135

90. Knackered – very tired, old or broken - 超劼，殘舊 / 很累   137

91. A pain (n) – something inconvenient, difficult to do - 真係麻煩 / 真是麻煩   138

92. Poorly (adj) / out of sorts / under the weather (adj phr) / run down (phr v) – not feeling well - 好差，唔舒服 / 很差，不舒服   140

93. Chop chop! – quickly -嗱嗱聲 - 快一點吧   141

94. Tacky - Cheap quality or in bad style - 好渣，寒酸/ 低俗，俗氣   142

95. It's dire! - it's bad, terrible, awful - 真係好屎/ 真是很差   143

96. Absolutely! / Of course! / Sure! – good! - 好！
當然啦！一定嘅！/ 行！　　　　　　　　　　　　　145

97. Brilliant! / Smashing! / Excellent! / Lovely! / Awesome! /
Beautiful! – very good - 好呀！超正呀！/ 極好！　　146

98. Sick! / appalling! / dreadful! / awful! / annoying! / a
nightmare! – very bad - 好差！恐怖！很差！　　　149

99. Crud! / Gross! – to refer to disgusting or unrefined
acts or things - 超核突！好肉酸！/ 很討厭的！很難看！　151

100. Flipping heck! (mildly rude) / Bloody hell! (rude) –
to express annoyance or anger - 頂佢吖！（少少俗），
（粗俗）/ 該死的！（粗俗）　　　　　　　　　　　152

101. For crying out loud! – to express annoyance - 激死喇！/
氣死了！　　　　　　　　　　　　　　　　　　　154

102. Give me a break! – stop doing / saying sth because it is
annoying or unbelievable (satirical) - 唔該你啦！（諷刺）/
別要這樣吧！（諷刺）　　　　　　　　　　　　　155

103. Have had it! – going to experience sth bad, unable to
accept a situation anymore - 玩完喇！夠喇！/ 玩完了！夠了！　157

104. Not give a monkey's! – not care about sth/sb, or not
interested at all - 話之佢！/ 不用理會！完全不在乎！　158

105. Oh my gosh (god)! / golly! – to express surprise,
excitement or fear - 哎喲！/ 我的天呀！　　　　　　161

106. What on earth?! / What the heck?! / What the hell?! –
words for emphasis (mildly rude) - 究竟？話之佢啦！
（少少俗）/ 搞什麼鬼？不用理會了！（少少俗）　　162

107. Have a go at someone - to criticize someone - 批評，指責　164

Chapter 4 To Tell Somebody Off　　　　　　　　166

xlv

108. Ask for it – to deserve something bad because sb didn't listen to advice – 攞嚟衰 / 自找麻煩	166
109. Bonkers / mental / (stark) raving mad / barmy (adj) / a basket case / a moron / a nutter (n) – crazy, out of sb's mind - 黐線，傻 / 瘋子，傻子(些粗俗)	167
110. A fibber (n) / tell fibs (v) – a liar, to tell lies about sth not too important - 講大話，大話精 / 撒謊的人	169
111. Give somebody an earful / give somebody a piece of one's mind – to tell sb you're very unhappy about sth/ sb - 鬧人（鬧死，爆）/ 罵人（罵死）(些粗俗)	170
112. Give somebody the two fingers / give somebody a bollocking – to express anger at sb (vulgar) - 問候佢，媽叉佢（超俗）/ 他媽的，咒罵（很粗俗）	171
113. Give someone a mouthful - to shout angrily at someone. (a little offensive) -媽叉，鬧人，罵人 (些粗俗)	172
114. Suck up to someone - to make someone like you by saying or doing something they like - 攞著數/取人便宜	174

Chapter 5 To Tease Somebody — 176

115. Cringe Cringe! – embarrassing - 好肉麻！/ 很肉麻！	176
116. Nice one! / That was clever! – you've done it badly / wrongly, that's the reason it's gone wrong (satirical) - 抵你死啦！你都好叻啫！（諷刺）/ 你應得的！你死定了！你都很聰明！（諷刺）	179
117. Over the top, OTT – exaggeration - 誇張	181
118. Take the mickey (To take the mick) – to make fun of someone - 笑人，玩人/取笑人，玩弄人	183
119. Wacky – (adj) funny, crazy - 搞笑，黐線 / 可笑的，瘋狂的	184

120. Take the piss (out of someone) (rude) - to make a joke or make someone look silly – 同人開玩笑/ 令人出醜 (粗俗) 186

Chapter 1

Everyday words and expressions

常用嘅字同講法

常用詞和常用語

1. A bit much – a bit unreasonable - 有啲過份/有些過份

e.g.SC: 2 friends talking over the phone:

e.g.SC(廣)：兩個朋友傾緊電話：

e.g.SC(普)：兩個朋友談電話：

A: How's Judy? I know you've broken up with her.

A: Judy 點呀？我知你同佢啱啱散咗喎！

A: Judy 好嗎？我知道你和他剛剛分了手！

B: She's not even talking to me now!

B: 佢而家仲唔同我講嘢添！

B: 他現在還沒有和我談話呀！

A: That's a bit much!

A: 咁佢有啲過分喇！

A: 他有些過分了！

e.g.SC: 2 ladies talking about another friend

A: I know Miriam has been on a diet. How's it going? Has she lost some weight yet?

A: 我知 Miriam 減緊肥喎！佢減成點呀？有冇輕咗呀？

A: 我知道 Miriam 正在減肥中，她減得怎麼樣啊？輕了沒有？

B: Yes, she's lost a stone in 4 weeks!

B: 有啊，佢喺四個星期內減咗 14 磅呀！

B: 有呀！她在 4 星期內減了 14 磅呀！

A: Amazing! How did she do it?

A: 正呀！佢點減架？

A: 很棒呀！她怎麼樣減呢？

B: I know she's been binging and purging!

B: 我知佢一直都會大飲大食，然後就扣喉，嘔返哂啲嘢出嚟。

B: 我知道他一直都在暴食，然後催吐。

A: That's a bit much! Quite dangerous really.

A: 嘩！咁真係有啲過份喎！仲幾危險添！

A: 嘩！真是有點過份！還很危險啊！

Break up = to end a relationship 分手. It can also mean the end of a school term 學期結束

Stone a measurement of weight in the UK = around 6 kg, or 14 pounds. 英國重量單位, 約 6 公斤, 約 14 磅, Singular noun 單數名詞. 1 stone, 2 stone.

Bingeing to binge is to eat a lot in a short period of time. Overeat. 大飲大食, 暴食

Purging to purge is to remove the food by throwing up. 嘔

To binge and purge an eating disorder that can lead to bulimia 貪食症

a bit of sth some, quite. 有啲, 有點 e.g. We may have a bit of a problem with the trains today. e.g. 我哋今日啲火車可能會有啲問題。我們今天的火車可能會有些問題。

Quite a sth to show sth/so is unusual 特別 e.g. I had quite a journey back to London. 我返去倫敦嘅旅程好特別。我有一個相當特別的旅程回倫敦。

2. Been there, done that – done sth before, experienced it before - 做過啦

e.g.SC: Some university Year 1 students asking for advice from the Year 2s:

e.g.SC: 大學 1 年級學生問緊 2 年級學生一啲貼士:

e.g.SC: 大學 1 年級學生向 2 年級學生徵求建議:

A: (Y1): So, we need to interview some bosses from different companies. What should we pay attention to?

A: (Y1): 我哋要 interview 啲公司老闆，咁要注意啲咩呀？

A: (Y1): 我們需要訪問一些公司的老闆，有什麼要注意呢？

B: (Y2): Oh been there, done that! – you should start by …

B: (Y2): 哦！做過依樣嘢啦！嗱你應該…

B: (Y2): 啊！已經做過了！你應該…

e.g.SC: 2 old friends planning a trip together

e.g.SC: 兩個老友計劃出 trip:

e.g.SC: 兩個老朋友計劃去旅行:

A: Do you want to backpack around Europe?

A: 想唔想去歐洲流浪呀？

A: 想不想去歐洲流浪呀？

B: Been there, done that. Let's do something more adventurous – mountain climbing in Nepal?

B: 做過啦！不如我哋做啲刺激啲嘅嘢吖！去尼泊爾爬山吖！

B: 做過了！我們做一些刺激的東西吧！去尼泊爾登山？

A backpack (n) a rugsack – a bag you carry on your back with straps on both shoulders. Also knapsack (US) 背囊背包

To backpack (v) – to travel around with such a bag, usually cheaply and with no extra luggage. 流浪

3. Bloke/ chap / guy – (US) (n) – a man – 男人

e.g.SC: 2 ladies talking:

e.g.SC: 兩個女人傾緊計:

e.g.SC: 兩個女人在聊天:

A: Who has that bloke you were going out with last night?

A: 尋晚同你出街嗰個男人喺邊個嚟㗎？

A: 昨晚和你出去的男人是誰呀？

B: Oh, just a friend from work.

B: 吓！公司啲 friend 嚟之嘛！

B: 啊！是朋友而已！

e.g.SC: 2 ladies talking:

e.g.SC: 兩個女人傾緊計:

e.g.SC: 兩個女人在聊天:

A: Do you remember the chap who came over to chat to us last week? He has rung me!

A: 喂！你記唔記得上個禮拜走過嚟同我哋傾計嗰個男人呀？佢有打電話比呀！

A: 喂！你記唔記得上個星期走過來和我們談話的男人呀？他打了電話給我啊！

B: Wow! Lucky you! He was gorgeous!

B: 嘩！你真係好彩！佢個樣都好 chok 㗎！

B: 嘩！你真是好運！他很英俊啊！

He's rung me (past tense) = he's called me (過去式) 佢打咗電話比我

4. Have a chat – talk about something casually - 傾下計 / 聊天

e.g. SC: A phones B:

e.g.SC: A 打電話比 B:

e.g.SC: A 打電話給 B:

A: Hey Sharon! Haven't seen you for a long time! Let's have coffee and have a chat.

A: 喂 Sharon，好耐冇見喎，出嚟飲杯咖啡，傾吓計吖！

A: Sharon，很久沒見了，出來喝咖啡，聊聊天吧！

B: Yeah, let's! I can do this week? How about you?

B: 好吖！我今個禮拜得閒，你呢？

B: 好呀！我這個星期有空，你呢？

e.g. SC: B is slightly unhappy. A goes over and asks:

e.g. SC: B 扁嘴，A 問:

e.g.SC: B 有些不開心，A 問:

A: Are you OK? Do you want a chat?

A: 你冇嘢啊嘛？！想唔想傾吓計呀？

A: 你沒有事嗎？想不想聊聊天呀？

B: That'd be good.

B: 嗯......好嘅。

B: 嗯......好呀。

I can do this week. I'm free this week; I can do the activity this week. 我今個禮拜得閒，我這個星期有空 It's also common to ask a question with 'can do'. e.g. Can you do this Friday? e.g. 你今個禮拜五得唔得/得唔得閒？你這個星期五可以嗎？有空嗎？

5. Cheers – thank you – 唔該/ 謝謝

e.g.SC: A house decorator asking his client B:

e.g.SC: 嗰裝修師傅，問緊啲客人:

e.g.SC: 裝修師傅問 B 客人:

A: Is this design what you wanted?

A: 嗰裝修啱唔啱心水呀？

A: 這個裝修你喜歡嗎？

B: Great! This is exactly what I wanted. Cheers!

B: 啱！依個就係我想要㗎喇！唔該！

B: 好！這個就是我想要的！謝謝！

e.g.SC: A buying B a drink at a pub.:

e.g.SC: 喺間酒吧度，A 買緊杯酒比 B:

e.g.SC: 在酒吧裏，A 正在買一杯酒給 B:

A: What would you like to drink?

A: 你想飲咩呀？

A: 你想喝什麼？

B: A glass of red please.

B: 紅酒吖，唔該！

B: 紅酒，謝謝！

A: Here you are (offering it to B).

A: 嗱！（比緊杯酒比 B）

8

A: 給你！（把酒拿給 B）

B: Cheers!

B: 唔該哂！

B: 謝謝!

Cheers can only mean 'thank you' in English, and not 'please'. 唔該 / 謝謝

Cheerio! Goodbye! 拜拜，再見

Cheers! It can mean a drinking toast 飲勝/乾杯

6. Chuck it / bin it / ditch it – (v) – to throw something away, to forget about it - 唔要，擱置/ 不要，擱置

e.g.SC: 2 designers talking about a design idea:

e.g.SC: 兩個設計師講緊一個設計嘅諗法:

e.g.SC: 兩個設計師正在討論一個設計的概念:

A: What do you think about these 2 drawings?

A: 依兩個設計圖你覺得點呀？

A: 這兩個設計圖你覺得怎麼樣呀？

B: Mmm… I'd bin this and keep this.

B: Mmm… 我唔會要依個，反而要 keep 返依個。

B: 嗯……我不想要這個，但想保留這個。

e.g.SC: 2 friends talking about their holiday plan:

e.g.SC: 兩個朋友講關於佢哋嘅度假計劃:

e.g.SC: 兩個朋友商量關於他們的度假計劃:

A: Peter, let's ditch this idea of going to Cambodia. I'm kind of tied up at the moment.

A: 喂，Peter! 都係擱置去柬埔寨喇！我而家真係行唔開！

A: 喂，Peter! 還是擱置去柬埔寨了！我現在真是走不開！

B: Are you sure mate? It's going to be a holiday of a lifetime!

B: 吓！（老友）你肯定？！一生人一次！一定要去下嘅！

B: 吓！（老兄）你肯定？！一生人一次吧！一定要去的！

To be tied up busy 唔得閒/ 很忙. **To be occupied** has the same meaning, but it's more for written English. 書寫用字

A mate (n) a causal word for a friend, usually used between 2 men. 老友 老兄. 男人之間朋友嘅稱呼 男人之間朋友的稱呼

7. Comfy – (adj) – comfortable - 舒服

e.g.SC: A couple choosing a bed at a bed store:

e.g.SC: 一對夫婦揀緊床上用品:

e.g.SC: 一對夫婦在床上用品店挑選中:

A: (wife): Darling, this bed is so comfy!

A:（老婆）：喂！老公呀！依張床褥好鬼死舒服喎！

A:（老婆）：喂！老公！這張床墊非常舒服啊！

B: (husband): Yeah – it's not bad!

B:（老公）：係喎老婆！唔錯喎！

B:（老公）：是我老婆！不錯喔！

e.g.SC: A boarding school teacher showing prospective parents what facilities the school has:

e.g.SC: 寄宿學校嘅老師帶啲家長去睇吓學校嘅環境同設施:

e.g.SC: 寄宿學校的老師大家長去看一下學校的環境和設施:

A: (teacher): …and in this common room, we have some comfy sofas and a communal TV.

A:（老師）：....仲有喺之間共用房度，我哋有啲好舒服嘅梳化同電視。

A:（老師）：還有在這間共用房中，我們有些好舒服的梳化和電視。

B: (parent): How often do the children get to come in here?

B:（家長）：啲細路仔可以隔幾耐用一次㗎？

B:（家長）：孩子可以多久用一次啊？

A: On Sundays usually.

A: 通常淨係星期日啫。

A: 通常只是星期天。

Another meaning of **comfortable** is to 'feel good/bad about doing something'. 覺得好 /唔係幾好 / 覺得好/不太好。

e.g. **I don't feel comfortable talking** to Diana about her problems. 我覺得同 Diana 講我哋啲問題唔係幾好。我覺得跟 Diana 說我們的問題不大好。

8. Dodgy – (adj) – very doubtful, suspicious - 好狡猾，懷疑，有啲問題/ 有些問題

e.g.SC: During 'happy hour' in a pub, colleagues A and B are talking about another colleague:

e.g.SC: 喺 happy hour 度，A 同事同 B 同事講:

e.g.SC: 在 happy hour，A 同事跟 B 同事說:

A: Patrick is kind of dodgy, be careful!

A: 喂！你小心啲呀 Patrick 呀，佢個人有啲狡猾㗎！

A: 喂！你要小心 Patrick 呀，他是一個有些狡猾的人啊！

B: Yeah – will do.

B: 係呀！會喇！

B: 是呀！會了！

e.g.SC: Coming out of a seafood restaurant, A is not feeling very well:

e.g.SC: A 喺海鮮酒家行出嚟，覺得唔舒服:

e.g.SC: A 從海鮮酒家走出來，覺得不舒服:

A: Oh – I feel sick! The prawns must have been dodgy!

A: 噢！我唔舒服呀！啲蝦一定有啲問題啦！

A: 噢！我不舒服呀！蝦一定有些問題呀！

B: Do you need to use their loo?

B: 咁你使唔使用佢哋個廁所呀？

B: 你要不要用他們的廁所嗎？

Kind of dodgy explained in this book

Shady (adj) dishonest, illegal 唔誠實，唔合法 不誠實，不合法

Will do! I will! 會喇！會了！

e.g. a **shady** character - 一個唔誠實嘅人 一個不誠實的人

loo explained in this book

9. Fags (n); Booze (n) – cigarettes - 煙仔 / 香煙; alcohol - 酒

e.g.SC: Some friends are organizing a leaving party:

e.g.SC: 一班朋友正在搞緊個歡送 party:

e.g.SC: 一班朋友正在安排一個送別 party:

A: Stacey likes jazz music, so let's get a jazz band, shall we?

A: Stacey 鍾意 jazz 音樂㗎！不如我哋去搵隊 jazz Band 返嚟啦！

A: Stacey 喜歡爵士音樂呀！我們去找一對爵士樂隊回來吧！

B: That sounds good. No fags allowed though – she hates fags, but plenty of booze!

B: 喂！好喎！不過食煙就唔准㗎啦，佢唔鍾意人食煙嘅，但係酒呢就好多都得！

B: 喂！好啊！不過哪裏不准抽煙的，她不喜歡別人抽煙，但是酒就可以喝多點！

e.g.SC: 2 friends are looking for a 7-11 that sells asthmatic medication:

e.g.SC: 兩個朋友去搵緊邊間七仔有哮喘藥賣:

e.g.SC: 兩個朋友去找哪一間 7-11 有哮喘藥賣:

A: Any luck with this one?

A: 依家有冇呀？

A: 這間有沒有呀？

B: Nope. Fags and booze – loads! Medicines – hardly any!

B: 冇呀！煙同走就好多！藥就好少喇！

B: 沒有呀！香煙和酒有很多，藥卻不多！

Any luck with sth? Have you succeeded in doing sth? 有冇運氣？做唔做到？有沒有運氣？做不做到？

Hardly any there's almost none. 好少 不多 It does not mean it's hard/difficult to have any

loads lots 好多 很多

hardly + verb almost can't do it. 做唔到 做不到

e.g. I can hardly eat anything right now – I'm so full from lunch! (= I can't eat anything right now)

e.g. 我而家咩都食唔落，食 lunch 食到好飽呀！我現在什麼都吃不下，lunch 吃得很飽啊！

Hardly + adj = not +adj 唔+ adj 不 + adj

e.g. It's hardly fair that they get some free gifts but we don't!

e.g. 佢哋有禮物，我哋冇，好唔公平姐！他們有禮物，我們沒有，很不公平啊！

Nope = No

10. Fancy doing something / Fancy something / someone (v) – like to do, like - 想做，鐘意/ 喜歡

e.g.SC: After school, at the school lobby:

e.g.SC: 放咗學，喺學校大堂:

e.g.SC: 放學後，在學校大堂裏:

A: What do you fancy doing now? Going for a walk?

A: 喂！你而家想做啲乜嘢呀？想唔想去行街？

A: 喂！你現在想做些什麼啊？想不想去散步嗎？

B: Yeah sure!

B: 好吖！

B: 好啊！

e.g.SC: Next to the lockers, at university:

e.g.SC: 大學裏邊 locker 嗰度:

e.g.SC: 在大學儲物室內:

A: I know you fancy Damien. Just come out with it now!

A: 喂！我知你鐘意 Damien，人少少認咗佢啦！

A: 喂！我知道你喜歡 Damien，認了它吧！

B: Damien! No way! He's so immature!

B: Damien! 冇可能啦！佢咁幼稚！

B: Damien! 不可能啦！他那麼幼稚！

fancy + v + **ing** sth/sb = to like doing sth 想做一啲嘢,想做一些事情

11. Get it – understand – 明白，收到

e.g.SC: Staff A tells staff B to do something:

e.g.SC: A 同事叫 B 同事做啲嘢:

e.g.SC: A 同事叫 B 同事做些事情:

A: Peter, remember to see Miss Leung when you go to Causeway Bay today.

A: 喂 Peter，你今日去銅鑼灣度，記住見梁小姐呀！

A: 喂 Peter，你今天去銅鑼灣，記得見梁小姐啊！

B: Got it!

B: 收到！

B: 明白！

e.g.SC: A's making a call to the mechanic B:

e.g.SC: A 部車攞咗去整，打緊電話去車房度:

e.g.SC: A 的車拿去修理，正在打電話給車房:

A: Hi, I'd like to pick up my car tomorrow.

A: 師傅，我部車聽日要攞㗎！

A: 師傅，我的車明天要取了！

B: Got it! It'll be ready tomorrow!

B: 收到！聽日攞得㗎喇！

B: 明白！明天可以取了！

This expression is usually said in the past tense **'got it'** because you must have understood it first before you say it so it must be in the past tense. 這個表達通常係用過去式，因為在回復之前你先已經理解請求。

It's different if it's a question. e.g. **Do you get it**? 除非係一個問題 - 你收唔收到？明唔明白？明不明白

To get it can also mean 'to be punished'. e.g. Thomas broke the vase! He's going to **get it**! e.g. Thomas 整爛個花樽！佢死喇！會比人罰喇！Thomas 弄破了花瓶！他死定了！他會給別人處罰的！

12. Have a go / It's somebody's go – have a try, sb's turn - 嘗試，到你喇 / 到你了

e.g.SC: At sports camp, learning high ropes

e.g.SC: 喺運動營裏面，學緊爬高繩：

e.g.SC: 在運動營內，正在學攀繩：

A: Peter, have a go! It won't hurt. You won't know unless you've tried.

A: Peter，試吓啦！唔使驚喎！你唔試吓點知唔得呢？！

A: Peter，試一下吧！不用害怕！至少你試過。

B: Do I really have to? Alright then (unwillingly).

B: 真係要？！唏....好啦....（死死氣）

B: 真是要嗎？！唉....好吧！....（不願意地）

e.g.SC: Playing a board game:

e.g.SC: 玩緊飛行棋：

e.g.SC: 正在玩棋子：

A: It's your go! Stop daydreaming!

A: 到你喇! 發晒夢！

A: 到你了！發白日夢！

B: Oh! – right, sorry. Your go now.

B: 哦，唔好意思呀！咁而家到你喇。

B: 啊！不好意思！現在到你了。

Right! = OK!

13. (It's a) good job (that)... – lucky – 好在/ 幸好..

e.g.SC: 2 girls talking about A's ex-boyfriend:

e.g.SC: 兩個女仔講緊 A 個 EX:

e.g.SC: 兩個女孩子說 A 的前任男友：

A: I just found out that Mark used to be a gang member!

A: 我啱啱先知道，原來阿 Mark 係黑社會成員嚟㗎！

A: 我剛剛才知道，原來 Mark 是黑社會成員呀！

B: It's a good job (that) you've broken up with him!

B: 你好在同佢散咗咋！

B: 你幸好和他分了手！

e.g.SC: Friends watching a fireworks display:

e.g.SC: 兩個朋友睇緊煙花：

e.g.SC: 兩個朋友看煙花：

A: Oh no! It's raining!

A: 唉呀！落雨呀！

A: 唉喲！下雨了！

B: Good job I've brought my umbrella!

B: 好在我有帶遮啫！

B: 幸好我有帶了傘子啊！

Ex-boyfriend a former boyfriend. Can also be shortened to 'ex/x' - 前男友。也可以縮寫為 'ex/x'

14. Grab some lunch / snack / have a bite to eat – get sth to eat - 去買啲嘢食 / 去買一些食物

e.g.SC: At school break, A talks to B:

e.g.SC: 喺學校小息度， A 同 B 講:

e.g.SC: 在學校小息中，A 跟 B 說:

A: Hey, just want to grab something to eat first – see you in the hall, ok?

A: 喂！去買啲嘢食先！一陣喺大堂度等吖！

A: 喂！我去買一些食物！在大堂等吧！

B: OK.

B: 好呀！

B: 好呀！

e.g.SC: 2 friends waiting for a bus:

e.g.SC: 兩個朋友等緊巴士:

e.g.SC: 兩個朋友正在等巴士:

A: I'm absolutely starving! I'll just pop across to grab a bite to eat first, ok?

A: 我好鬼肚餓呀！我過對面去買啲嘢食先。

A: 我很餓呀！我去買一些小吃。

B: Ok – oh can you grab me a sandwich? And some of those little eggie cakes please?

B: 好呀 - 喂幫我買份三文治吖，同埋一份雞蛋仔呀唔該！

B: 好呀！幫我買一份三文治和一份雞蛋仔，謝謝！

a bite to eat usually a small meal, small amount of food = a snack/snacks 小食 小吃

grub/chow food 嘢食 食物

starving very hungry 很餓

pop across explained in this book

sandwich can be shortened to 'sani' 可以縮寫為"sani"

15. To be honest / Honestly! (adv) – actually, to tell you the truth, please don't do that! (embarrassing) - 講真吖，唔係咁下話（尷尬）/真心話，不是這樣的嗎？

e.g.SC: Two students talking about the tutorial that evening:

e.g.SC: 兩個大學生，傾緊嗰晚嘅 Tutorial:

e.g.SC: 兩個大學生，正在討論那晚的課：

A: Hey, are you going to Dr. Cheng's tutorial this evening?

A: 喂！你今晚去唔去 Dr. Cheng 嗰 Tutorial 呀？

A: 喂！你今晚晚上上不上 Dr.Cheng 的課啊？

B: I don't really want to go. To be honest, it's gonna be a waste of time!

B: 唉！我真係唔想去。講真吖，啲 Tutorial 都冇乜用，嘥氣啦！

B: 唉！我真是不想去。真心話，所有的課都沒有用的，浪費時間！

e.g.SC: 2 grown-up girls waiting for a bus at a bus stop. A shows B her wallet with a 'hello kitty' design on it:

e.g.SC: 兩個女仔喺度等緊巴士，A 攞住佢嘅'Hello Kitty'銀包同 B 講：

e.g.SC: 兩個女孩子在等巴士，A 拿着 'Hello Kitty'錢包跟 B 說：

A: Look at my new wallet!

A: 喂！你睇吓我個新銀包！

A: 喂！你看我這個新銀包！

B: Honestly! How old are you?

B: 喂！你唔係下話……你幾歲呀？

B: 喂！你不是這樣的嗎……你幾歲呀？

is gonna be oral form of 'is going to be' 口頭形式的 '將會是'

Honestly! Tone for this word should be a '**down**' tone on the 'ly' to show sarcasm. 音調 - 喺 ly 低音表達諷刺

16. Idea / clue (n) – know 知

e.g.SC: A is on his iPhone. Suddenly the phone has frozen:

e.g.SC: A 用緊，突然間個 iPhone 唔 work：

e.g.SC: A 正在用 iPhone，iPhone 突然當機了：

A: Flipping heck! The iPhone's frozen! I was in the middle of chatting with Jonathan on Facebook! What's wrong with it?

A: 頂！個 iPhone 唔 work 呀！唉！我同緊 Jonathan 喺 Facebook 度吹緊水㗎！點解會咁嘅？

A: 搞什麼鬼！個 iPhone 停了！唉！我正在和 Jonathan 在 Facebook 中聊天呀！為什麼會這樣的？

B: (taking phone from A to have a look) No idea! Google it to find a fix!

B:（攞咗 A 電話睇吓）唔知呢！上 Google 搵吓點樣整返佢啦！

B:（拿了 A 電話看）不知道啊！用 Google 找一下怎樣去修理吧！

e.g.SC: In a kitchen. A says to B:

e.g.SC: 喺廚房度，A 同 B 講：

e.g.SC: 在廚房裏，A 跟 B 說：

A: Now we fry the vegetables first, then do the beef.

A: 嗱！而家我哋炒啲菜先，跟住炒牛肉。

A: 嗱！現在我們炒菜，然後炒牛肉。

B: What! The beef should go in first, shouldn't it? You don't seem to have any clue about cooking!

B: 咩！牛肉唔係炒先咩？！你好似完全唔知點煮嘢食咁喎！

B: 什麼！首先不是炒牛肉嗎？你好像完全不知道烹調方法啊！

Has frozen: stopped working 停止工作

Flipping heck: explained in this book

Also – **go dead** – not working 唔 work 停了

e.g. The iPhone **has gone dead** (on me – optional). e.g. 個 iPhone 死咗機。當機了

Have + any idea

A: e.g. Do you have any idea about how long it takes to get to the airport?

A: e.g. 你知唔知去機場要幾耐？你知不知道去機場需要多少時間？

B: (I have) no idea!

B: 唔知喎！不知道！

17. Kind of / sort of – quite (transition words) - 幾（過渡詞）/ 有點兒

e.g.SC: 2 teenage girls are chatting:

e.g.SC: 兩個後生女傾緊計：

e.g.SC: 兩個年青女孩子正在聊天：

A: So did you like that movie?

A: 咁你鍾唔鍾意嗰套戲呀？

A: 你喜歡那套電影嗎？

B: It was sort of nice, but the ending was crap!

B: 都幾好嘅！不過收尾就差到爆喇！

B: 還好吧！不過結局不行！

e.g.SC: 2 friends chatting:

e.g.SC: 兩個朋友傾緊計：

e.g.SC: 兩個朋友正在聊天：

A: So how do you like being called 'a big spender'?

A: 你比人叫'大闊佬'咁你覺得點呀？

A: 他們叫你'大款/闊爺' 你覺得怎麼樣呢？

B: I kind of feel proud about it, for some strange reason.

B: 有陣時我都幾自豪㗎！

B: 有時候我會有點兒自豪的啊！

Crap explained in this book

18. Knick (v) – steal 偷

e.g.SC: At a soccer pitch, after a match:

e.g.SC: 比賽完，喺足球場度：

e.g.SC: 比賽完了，足球場裏：

A: Where's my phone? I left it on the bench! It's been knicked!

A: 我個電話呢我留咗喺張凳度呀！哎呀！俾人偷咗呀！

A: 我的電話呢？我樓下了在椅子上呀！哎呀！比人偷了！

B: Told you to keep it in the locker!

B: 話咗你要 keep 喺 locker 度㗎啦！

B: 跟你說過要放在儲物櫃裏面的！

e.g.SC: At school, in the classroom:

e.g.SC: 喺學校班房度：

e.g.SC: 在學校教室內：

A: Don't leave your laptop in the classroom - it might get knicked!

A: 你千祈唔好留低，你個 laptop 喺班房度呀！實會有人偷㗎！

A: 你千萬不要留下你的手提電腦，在教室裏面的啊！一定會被別人偷的！

B: Oh yeah. You're right!

B: 吖！係呀！

B: 對啊！

In these examples, "**get knicked**" is in the **passive** voice. 俾人偷咗 被別人偷了

19. Leg it (v) – to run, to run away from sth/sb - 閃，閃避/ 走，走避

e.g.SC: At the office at 5:02 pm, the manager comes out of his office:

e.g.SC: 喺 office，經理喺 5:02PM 行出嚟：

e.g.SC: 在 office 裏，經理在 5:02PM 走出來：

A: (manager): Where's everyone?

A:（經理）：啲人去晒邊呀？

A:（經理）：所有人去了哪裏啊？

B: (supervisor): They've all legged it out of the office at 5 sharp!

B:（主任）：佢哋一到 5:00 就即閃喇！

B:（主任）：他們一到五點就走了吧！

e.g.SC: At the bus stop. A sees B, who's supposed to have waited for her:

e.g.SC: 喺巴士站度，B 應該要等 A。

e.g.SC: A 見到 B：在巴士站，B 應該要等 A。A 看見 B：

A: Where were you?

A: 你頭先喺邊呀？

A: 你剛剛在哪裏？

B: Sorry I should've waited for you, but I saw Jerry coming my way so I legged it. You know I don't want to see that jerk!

B: Sorry 呀！我應該要等你先嘅，不過見到 Jerry 行緊過嚟，咁我咪即閃囉！你知我唔想見到嗰個衰人㗎喇！

B: 對不起！我應該要等你，不過我見到 Jerry 行過來，我就避開了！你知道我不想見到那個混蛋的吧！

<u>jerk</u> explained in this book

20. Like – transition word when thinking what to say next - 就話，咁，就，諗緊同事（過渡詞）

e.g.SC: On the tube, 2 students talking:

e.g.SC: 兩個學生搭緊地鐵：

e.g.SC: 兩個學生坐地鐵：

A: ……She was trying to change back to her school shoes, but she realized they were gone!

A: ……佢想去玩返對返學鞋，但係佢知道對鞋已經冇咗！

A: ……他想玩想他的學校鞋子，但是他知道鞋子已經不見了！

B: Really! So what did she do? (laughing)

B: 真係！咁佢點呀？（笑住）

B: 真的嗎！她怎樣呀？（笑着）

A: She was mad! She was like, "It's not funny – who took my shoes!"

A: 佢嬲到爆囉！！咁佢就話'唔好玩啦！邊個攞咗我對鞋呀？！'

A: 她很怒！！她就說'不好玩呀！誰拿了我的鞋子呀？！'

e.g.SC: In a park, 2 friends are chatting about somebody trying to smuggle a little dog into a residential block:

e.g.SC: 喺公園度，兩個朋友傾緊關於有個朋友想偷隻狗仔入大廈裏面：

e.g.SC: 在公園裏，兩個朋友討論某人想偷運一隻狗兒進入大廈：

A: ……Pat didn't realise the security guard was standing right behind her!

A: …… Pat 完全唔知道'食Q'就企喺佢後面！

A: …… Pat 完全不知道警衛就站在他後面！

B: Oh no! So what happened?

B: O……NO！咁跟住點呀？

B: 然後如何啊？

A: I was like, winking at her, to let her know the security guard was there. She had no idea what I was trying to do! She was like "What's wrong with your eye?"

A: 我就同佢打眼色，想俾佢知嗰'食 Q '企喺佢後面。但係佢完全唔知我做緊咩！佢就講'做咩你隻眼？'

A: 我向她眨眼，想讓他知道警衛在她後面。但是她完全不知道我在幹嘛！她就說'你的眼睛沒有事嗎？'

Mad (adj) angry 嬲 怒

Difference between 'know' and 'realise' 分別

Know (v) to have information because you've been told or have learnt about it. 知道

e.g. I know he's coming today – Amanda told me. e.g. - 我知佢今日會嚟 - Amanda 話我知。我知道她今天會來 - Amanda 告訴我的。

Realise (v)– to understand or become aware of sth. 領悟

e.g. I've come to **realize** something now that I'm older: that age doesn't matter!

e.g. 我而家年紀大咗喇，先至領悟到一件事-年齡係唔緊要嘅！我現在年紀大了才明白一件事-年齡是不重要的！

21. Go to the loo / desperate for the loo / desperate for a pee (mildly rude) – go to toilet, want to go to the toilet badly - 去廁所，好想去廁所，好急尿（少少俗）/撒尿

e.g.SC: At the train station, about to get on the train:

e.g.SC: 喺火車站到上緊車嗰時：

e.g.SC: 在火車站，正在上車時：

A: Hang on, I'm desperate for the loo. Wait here!

A: 喂！等陣先啦，好想去廁所呀！等埋我呀！

A: 喂！等一等！我很想上廁所啊！等我！

B: Oh! Why didn't you go earlier? Hurry! The train's leaving!

B: 唉呀！早啲又唔去，快啲啦！火車就嚟開喇！

B: 哎喲！早一點你不去，快！火車差不多開了！

e.g.SC: Two men in the car, B driving:

e.g.SC: 兩個男人喺車裏面，B揸緊車：

e.g.SC: 兩個男人在車裏面，B正在開車：

A: I'm desperate for a pee!

A: 我好急尿呀！

A: 我要撒尿啊！

B: Want me to pull over just in front there?

B: 想唔想我喺前面停一停呀？

B: 想不想我在前邊停一停嗎？

Hang on - wait 等 , **the loo** - the toilet 廁所

22. No problem / no worries – it's ok - 冇問題/沒有問題

e.g.SC: At university, in the classroom:

e.g.SC: 喺大學，課室裏面：

e.g.SC: 大學教室裏：

A: Hey Sandy, thanks for writing this up. The presentation is gonna be great!

A: 喂 Sandy，唔該晒你幫我寫咗篇嘢，個 presentation 一定會好好㗎！

A: Sandy，謝謝你幫我寫了這篇文章。這報告一定會很好的！

B: No problem!

B: 哦！冇問題！

B: 沒有問題！

e.g.SC: At Starbucks, A worrying about B's car:

e.g.SC: 喺 Starbucks 度，A 擔心緊 B 架車：

e.g.SC: 在 Starbucks，A 正在擔心 B 的車：

A: Is it OK to park your car right outside for so long? It's not a proper place!

A: 喂！你架車泊喺依度咁耐，又唔係泊車位，得唔得㗎？

A: 喂！你的車停在這裏那麼久，又不是停車位，可不可以的？

B: No worries! I always park here!

B: OK 㗎，冇問題！我成日都係咁泊㗎啦！

B: 沒有問題！我常常都是這樣停的。

23. Pop – go somewhere quickly for a short time (v) - 過一過嚟，入一入嚟/ 過一過來，入一入來

e.g.SC: 2 neighbours talking, standing close to B's house:

e.g.SC: 兩個鄰居，企咗喺 B 屋企附近傾緊計：

e.g.SC: 兩個鄰居，站在近 B 的家談話：

A: I'll pop round later to pick up that cake, is that alright?

A: 喂！我一陣過一過嚟，攞你個蛋糕，得唔得呀？

A: 喂！我稍後過來，拿你這個蛋糕，可不可以嗎？

B: Yeah sure – no problem.

B: 冇問題。

B: 沒有問題。

e.g.SC: 2 people cooking:

e.g.SC: 兩個人煮緊嘢食：

e.g.SC: 兩個人在烹調中：

A: Just pop it in the oven, and we're done!

A: 放咗入去焗爐到，就搞掂㗎喇！

A: 放在焗爐內，就完成了！

B: It'd better be good!

B: 係好食先好呀！

B: 好吃才說吧！

Pop + prep (round/over/across)

Also pop + preposition + sw 放一啲嘢去一個地方 放一些東西在一個地方

It'd better be good: has the feeling that the speaker has put a lot of effort into it. If it doesn't turn out well, the speaker will be upset or disappointed. So it expresses more expectation (and possible frustration) than "**I hope it's good**". "It'd better be good" 多期望過 "I hope it's good".

It'd better be **good**! The stress should be on the words "better" and "good" to bring out the feeling of expectancy. 語氣，音調 - 喺 "better" 同 "good" 加重表達期望。在 better 和 good 加重表達期望。

24. Quid (n) – sterling pound - 英鎊

e.g.SC: At the supermarket car park ticket machine:

e.g.SC: 喺超級市場嘅停車場，個收銀機度：

e.g.SC: 超級市場的停車場內，收銀機處：

A: The parking is 2 quid for 2 hours – do you have 2 quid?

A: 泊車兩個鐘，要兩磅，咁你有冇兩磅呀？

A: 泊車兩個小時要兩磅，你有沒有兩磅啊？

B: Let me check. Here you go!

B: 等我睇吓……嗱！

B: 讓我看看……嗱！

e.g.SC: At a farmer's market:

e.g.SC: 喺街市度：

e.g.SC: 在街市內：

A: A quid for a kilo of broccoli – wow! That's cheap!

A: 嘩！一斤西蘭花！真係好平喎！

A: 嘩！一磅一斤西蘭花！真是好便宜呀！

B: Yeah – the farmers must have had a good harvest this year!

B: 係呀！今年啲農夫有好多收成呀！

B: 對啊！今年的農夫收成很好啊！

Here you go = here it is 嗱,在這裡

Quid does not have a plural form. One quid, two quid. Quid 係冇複數 是沒有複數的 一磅 兩磅

25. Reckon (v) – think - 諗，覺得

e.g.SC: 2 friends driving, trying to find the way:

e.g.SC: 兩個朋友揸緊車，搵緊路：

e.g.SC: 兩個朋友正在開車找路：

A: I reckon we need to do a right here.

A: 我諗我哋要轉右。

A: 我覺得我們要右拐。

B: Think a left…

B: 我諗係左……

B: 我覺得左邊……

e.g.SC: A and B having dinner in a restaurant:

e.g.SC: A 同 B 食緊晚飯：

e.g.SC: A 和 B 正在吃晚飯：

A: The food's quite good here. What do you reckon?

A: 我覺得依間啲嘢食都唔錯呀！你覺得呢？

A: 我覺得這間的食物都相當不錯。你覺得呢？

B: Mmm… it's ok… (sounding unimpressed)

B: OK 啦！過得去囉…（覺得唔係幾好）

B: OK 啦！還可以吧…（覺得不太好）

<u>It's ok</u> … - it's only ok, not that great. 過得去, 唔係幾好　還可以, 不太好

26. Let's rock and roll (let's roll)! – eager to start to do sth - 迫不及待想去做

e.g.SC: After school, student A says to student B excitedly:

e.g.SC: 放學後，A 同學同 B 同學好開心咁講：

e.g.SC: 放學後，A 同學跟 B 同學很開心地說：

A: Hey, do you want to grab a bite to eat before home?

A: 喂！去食啲嘢先返屋企啦！

A: 喂！吃點東西才回家吧！

B: Sure!!

B: 好呀！

B: 好啊！

A: Yeah! Let's rock and roll!!

A: 我哋去喇！！

A: 我們去吧！！

e.g.SC: At the end of dinner, leaving the restaurant:

e.g.SC: 食完飯，正在離開餐廳：

e.g.SC: 食飯後，正在離開餐廳：

A: One for the road?

A: 去飲多一杯先走啦！

A: 多喝一杯酒才走吧！

B: Sure! A nightcap sounds good.

B: 好呀！飲多一杯先瞓囉。

B: 好啊！多喝一杯酒才睡覺吧。

A: Let's roll!!

A: 去喇！

A: 去吧！

Grab a bite explained in this book

Sure = ok

Let's rock and roll! – can be shortened to "**Let's roll**" 去喇！去吧！

A pub crawl – a British hobby – to visit several pubs, one after another, drinking at each one of them. 去完一間 PUB 又去另一間 PUB（走場）

One for the road – to have one more glass of alcohol before sb leaves a place. 去飲多一杯先走 多喝一杯酒才走

A nightcap – to have a glass of alcohol before sleep. 飲多一杯先瞓 多喝一杯酒才睡覺

27. Sorted / sort something out / get sorted – problem solved, solve the problem, get organized - 搞掂，搞掂一個問題，搞返掂佢/收拾，解決了問題

e.g.SC: At university, 2 students planning for the next presentation:

e.g.SC: 喺大學兩個學生計劃緊下個 presentation：

e.g.SC: 在大學兩個學生正在計劃下一個報告：

A: This paragraph is too long. You need to shorten it. Can you sort it out by Friday?

A: 依段太長喇！你要簡短啲喇！星期五前搞唔搞得掂？

A: 依段太長喇！你要簡短啲喇！星期五前搞唔搞得掂？

B: OK, no problem.

B: OK，冇問題。

B: 沒有問題。

On Friday, B says to A: 星期五，B 同 A 講：星期五，B 同 A 說：

B: Sorted! It's much shorter now. Have a look!

B: 搞掂咗喇！短咗好多喇。你睇吓！

B: 收拾好了！短了很多，你看看吧！

e.g.SC: At boarding school, inside dormitory:

e.g.SC: 喺寄宿學校，大房裏面：

e.g.SC: 在寄宿學校，大房裏面：

A: Look at this mess! Sort yourself out mate, or I won't share the dorm with you!

A: 嘩！你啲嘢咁亂嘅，你唔搞番掂佢，我就唔同你 SHARE 間房㗎啦！

A: 嘩！你的東西非常亂啊，如果你不收拾收拾，我就不跟你住在一起！

B: It's an organized mess! Fine! I'll tidy it. Don't tell!

B: 唔係好亂啫！算啦，唏！我會執執佢㗎喇！嗱！唔好報串呀！！

B: 不是很亂啊！算了，唉！我會收拾一下。你不好報告啊！

To tell on sb to let sb else know about their secret 報串，報告秘密

28. That'll do –it's enough - 都夠㗎喇，唔使再做，講/ 足夠，不用再做，說

e.g.SC: In the manager's office. The supervisor is trying to tell B the manager what had happened in the office when he was away:

e.g.SC: 喺經理室度，A 主任同緊 B 經理講，當經理唔喺度嗰陣時，office 發生咗咩事：

e.g.SC: 在經理室內，A 主任和 B 經理說經理不在的時候，辦公室發生了什麼事：

A: Boss, Sammy was 8 minutes late on Wednesday, Florence left 5 minutes early on Thursday, On Friday, Vivienne fell sick and…

A: 經理，星期三，Sammy 遲到 8 分鐘。星期四 Florence 早走 5 分鐘，星期五 Vivienne 就唔舒服….

A: 經理，星期三，Sammy 遲到 8 分鐘。星期四 Florence 早退 5 分鐘，星期五 Vivienne 就不舒服….

B: That'll do Francis. I'll look into those irregularities in my own time.

B: 唔使再講喇 Francis。我自己有時間嘅時候會跟番啲嘢㗎喇！

B: 不用在說 Francis。我自己有時間的時候會跟進這些事情的！

e.g.SC: A has invited B to his house for dinner:

e.g.SC: A 被邀請去 B 屋企食晚飯：

e.g.SC: A 被邀請去 B 家裏吃晚飯：

A: (pilling a whole load of peas onto B's plate): Fancy some peas?

A:（放咗好多青豆喺 B 隻碟度）：想唔想要啲青豆呀？

A:（放了很多青豆在 B 碟上）：想不想要點青豆嗎？

B: That'll do for now James, thanks.

B: 都夠㗎喇！唔該晒 James！

B: 足夠了！謝謝 James！

"**That'll do**" – we should have a down tone for 'do' to express you've had enough of sth 音調- 喺 **DO** 低音，表達「已經夠喇」DO 音調低，表達「已經足夠了」。

Whole load of = a lot of 很多

Fancy some peas - explained in this book

29. Tricky (adj) – problematic, difficult to do - 難啲喎/難處理的

e.g.SC: A boy inviting a girl to have dinner with him:

e.g.SC: 嗰男仔約緊嗰女仔去食飯：

e.g.SC: 男孩約一個女孩去吃飯：

A: Wanna have dinner with me this Friday?

A: 今個禮拜五你想唔想同我去食飯呀？

A: 這個星期五你想唔想跟我去食飯嗎？

B: Friday's tricky – I'm afraid I can't!

B: 禮拜五難啲喎！我諗我唔得喇！

B: 星期五很難啊！大概不行了！

e.g.SC: A supervisor's talking to his worker:

e.g.SC: A 主任問佢下屬講緊：

e.g.SC: A 主任，跟他的下屬說：

A: (supervisor): John's on leave till next month. We need you to come and start work at 8 am, from tomorrow, to cover for him. Is that alright?

A:（主任）：阿 John 而家放緊假，至到下個月。咁我哋要你 cover 做佢啲嘢，你聽日開始返 8 點，有冇問題？

A: John 現在放假中，下個月才回來。我們需要你承擔他的工作，你明天開始八點上班，有沒有問題？

B: That's tricky Boss. I have to take my daughter to school every morning…

B: 依個難啲喎波士！我每朝都一定要帶我嘅女去返學㗎……

B: 這個難一點吧老闆！我每天都一定要帶我的女兒上學去的……

30. We'll see, won't we (Q tag) – see how the situation develops - 到時咪知囉，睇吓點/看看吧

e.g.SC: 2 colleagues talking about their pay:

e.g.SC: 兩個同事講緊薪金嘅嘢：

e.g.SC: 兩名同事正在說薪金的事情：

A: I wonder if we'll have our year-end bonus this year. The economy has been so bad!

A: 唉！唔知今年有冇花紅呢？今年經濟咁差！

A: 唉！不知道今年有沒有花紅呢？今年經濟很差啊！

B: We'll see, won't we?

B: 到時睇吓點！

B: 走著瞧吧！

e.g.SC: 2 parents talking about their child's school report:

e.g.SC: 兩個家長講緊佢哋啲細蚊仔學校成績表：

e.g.SC: 兩個家長再談他們的小孩子學校成績報告：

A: I wonder what grade Cindy will get in Maths this term. She's not keen on Maths at all!

A: 唉！我諗緊 Cindy 啲數學今年會考成點呢？佢真係唔鍾意數學㗎！,

A: 唉！我想 Cindy 的數學科成績怎麼樣呢？她真的不喜歡數學她的！

B: We'll see when the report card comes through, won't we?

B: 張成績表出咗嚟嗰時就知囉！

B: 當成績報告出來的時候再看吧！

keen on = like 鍾意 喜歡

31. Whatever – however sb likes it - 是但啦 / 沒有所謂

e.g.SC: At the café:

e.g.SC: 喺間茶餐廳度：

e.g.SC: 在茶餐廳內：

A: Hey, do you want to have: French toast or pineapple bun?

A: 喂！你想食西多士定係菠蘿包呀？

A: 喂！你想吃西多士還是菠蘿包啊？

B: Whatever – French toast then.

B: 是但啦！西多士啦囉!

B: 沒有所謂！西多士吧！

e.g.SC: 2 children begging mum to buy something:

e.g.SC: 兩個細路煩緊媽咪買嘢：

e.g.SC: 兩個小孩煩着媽媽買東西：

A: (child): Oh Mum, please, we really want the game! Please get it, please!

A:（仔）：媽咪，我哋好想要依隻 game 呀！買啦！買俾我哋啦！

A: 媽媽，我們很想要這電腦遊戲啊，買給我們吧！

B: (child): Yeah mum, we promise to be really good!

B:（仔）：係呀媽咪！我哋應承你一定會好乖㗎！

B: 對啊，媽媽！我們答應你一定會很乖的！

C: Mum (feels annoyed – sighs) Whatever!

C:（媽）（好煩）：唏！是但啦！

C: 唏！沒有所謂吧！

32. What have you / what not – whatever else, 'etc' - 嗰啲嘢 / 那些東西

e.g.SC: A mother trying to tell his teenage son to get ready to go out:

e.g.SC: 媽咪叫個仔去準備出街：

e.g.SC: 媽媽叫他的兒子去準備上街：

A: Harry, you need to get ready – turn off the computer, T.V. and what have you.

A: Harry！你要去準備喇！去熄咗電視，電腦嗰啲嘢啦！

A: Harry！你要去準備吧！去關掉電視，電腦那些東西吧！

B: OK mum!

B: OK 媽咪！

B: 好的，媽媽！

e.g.SC: 2 friends trying to get things together for a picnic on the beach:

e.g.SC: 兩個朋友執緊啲嘢去海灘食午餐：

e.g.SC: 兩個朋友正在執拾一些東西去海灘吃午餐：

A: Now what do we need to pack?

A: 喂！我哋需要帶啲咩？

A: 喂！我們需要帶什麼東西呢？

B: Knives, forks, tissues, what not.

B: 刀，叉，紙巾嗰啲嘢囉！

B: 刀子，叉子，紙巾那些東西吧！

'What have you'/'what not' – the speaker knows the other person understands what those things are, so it's unnecessary to list them all.
嗰啲嘢 那些東西

33. What're you up to? What's up with you? How's it going? (Q) – greeting - 最近點呀？/ 近來怎麼樣啊？

e.g.SC: At a student reunion dinner:

e.g.SC: 喺學生聚餐會：

e.g.SC: 在學生聚餐會裏：

A: Hey Patsy, I haven't seen you for ages! What're you up to these days?

A: 喂！Patsy，好耐冇見喇喎！你最近點呀？

A: 喂！Patsy，好久不見！你近來怎麼樣啊？

B: Oh! Hi Heidi! Wow! It's been a while! I'm fine…just preparing for a job interview with HSBC at the moment. Did you know I resigned from Citibank?

B: 噢！Hi Heidi！真係好耐冇見喎！我 OK 呀！我預備緊同 HSBC 嗰 interview。喂，你知我冇做 Citibank 㗎啦？

B: 噢！Hi Heidi！真是好久不見啊！我不錯呀！我預備和 HSBC 的面試。喂，你知道我沒有在 Citibank 上班了嗎？

e.g.SC: At a coffee shop, A brings over coffee to B:

e.g.SC: 喺 coffee shop 度，A 攞緊杯 coffee 俾 B：

e.g.SC: 在咖啡廳裏，A 正拿着一杯咖啡給 B：

A: So, what's up with you lately?

A: 喂！你最近點呀？

A: 喂！你近來怎麼樣啊？

B: Nothing really. Much the same. How about you?

B: 冇呀！又係咁啦！你呢？

B: 沒有什麼啊！都是一樣吧！你呢？

For ages =for a long time - 很長一段時間

Prepare + for + sth = to get ready for sth 準備一啲嘢 準備一些東西 **but**

To prepare + lunch/dinner (No need to add 'for') 預備午餐/晚餐 (唔需要 for)

Two weeks **ago**, BUT **since** last week, **not** last week ago. – **ago** 同 **since** 嘅分別 ago 和 since 的分別

A positive response to greetings could be: **"I'm pretty good!"** 我幾好呀！

Lately = recently 最近 近來

34. Swamped (adj) –overwhelmed 冧檔 - 超忙 - 很忙

e.g.SC: You work at a local restaurant. It's your day off so you're meeting a friend. Suddenly your phone rings:

e.g.SC: 你喺茶餐廳打工。今日你放假，諗住想約朋友之際，突然你手機電話响：

e.g.SC: 你是茶餐廳的侍應生。今天你正在放假，而且想相約朋友的時候，突然你手機電話正在響：

A: Hello?

A: 喂？

B: Hey Ricky, we're swamped right now! Is it possible for you to come back and help out now?

B: 喂 Ricky，我哋餐廳冧晒檔呀！你可唔可以而家即刻返嚟幫手？

B: 喂 Ricky，我們的餐廳很忙啊！你可不可以現在立刻回來幫手？

A: Boss, it's my day off today But yeah ok, I'll try and be back by 1pm.

A: 老細，今日我放假喎！但係 OK 啦，咁我試吓一點返到嚟。

A: 老闆，今天是我的假期啊！但是可以的，我嘗試一點回來吧！

e.g.SC: 2 friends chatting:

e.g.SC: 兩個朋友傾緊計：

e.g.SC: 兩個朋友傾談中：

A: How are you doing lately Magnus? You said you were going for a holiday soon!

A: Magnus 你最近點呀？你唔係話好快去旅行咩？

A: Magnus 你最近好嗎？你不是說過很快去旅行嗎？

B: I've been so swamped with work! Not a moment to even think about a holiday!!

B: 我呢排忙到死囉！而家我都冇時間去諗去旅行呀！！

B: 最近我很忙啊！我仍沒有時間去想去旅行呢！！

35. A walk in the park -an easy thing to do - 超易, 很容易的

e.g.SC: A supervisor is teaching a staff member how to enter data onto the computer:

e.g.SC: 主任教緊員工點樣入數據喺電腦度：

e.g.SC: 主任正在校員工怎樣入數據在電腦裏：

A (supervisor): Now you start by pressing this button here, then you…… Can you do it?

A:（主任）：嗱！而家你開始可以喺度撳呢度。跟住你……你做唔做到先？

A:（主任）： 現在你開始可以在這裏按這個鍵。然後你… 你做不做到？

B (staff): No problem boss! It's a walk in the park!

B:（員工）：掂呀！老細，呢個超易呀！

B:（員工）：可以啊！老闆！這個很容易的！

e.g.SC: A mother is asking her son to look after the cat while she is away for a short break:

e.g.SC: 媽咪問緊個仔可唔可以佢旅行嘅時候照顧隻貓貓：

e.g.SC: 媽媽正在問她的兒子可不可以當她旅行的時候照顧貓貓：

A (mother): Feed him twice a day, half a cup each time. Change the litter once every 3-4 days. Are you ok with that?

A:（媽咪）：餵佢一日兩次，每次半杯。換貓砂三四日一次，你得唔得先？

A:（媽媽）：一日兩次餵食，每次半杯。更換貓砂 3-四日一次，你可不可以？

B (son): Don't worry mum! It's a walk in the park. Just go and enjoy yourself!

B:（仔）：唔使擔心啦媽咪！呢個超易做！你玩得開心啲啦！

B:（兒子）：不用擔心吧媽媽！這個很容易做的！你開心玩吧！

Some may like to say '**easy peasy**', which has the same meaning.

e.g. with the example above, the son could say:

Don't worry mum! It's easy peasy! Just go and enjoy yourself!

有些人可能喜歡說 'easy peasy'，這有同樣的意思。

例如 透過上面的例子，兒子可以說：

別擔心媽媽！這很容易！你開心玩吧！

36. The real deal - someone or something that is very good and has the qualities that people say they have - 堅嘢，超勁, 真貨，很勁

e.g.SC: At Five Guys Hamburger's:

e.g.SC: 喺一間漢堡包店：

e.g.SC: 在一間漢堡包店裏：

A: Hey they have Smoked Chilli Chicken on the menu today: it's the real deal you know!

A: 喂！佢哋今日首選有煙燻雞：真係堅㗎！

A: 喂！他們今日首選是煙燻雞！真是真貨的！

B: Wow, I'll go for this!

B: 嘩！我要叫依個！

B: 噢！我要點這個！

e.g.SC: At a parent's music night at school. One parent is commenting on the child pianist who's playing:

e.g.SC: 喺學校家長音樂晚會度，有一個家長喺度評論嗰個彈緊琴嘅細佬仔：

e.g.SC: 在學校的家長音樂之夜。一位家長正在評論在演奏的兒童鋼琴家：

A: He's the real deal! Excellent performance!

A: 佢真係彈得超正！表演真係勁！

A: 他真是彈得很好！表演十分精彩！

B: Yes, I agree, very well done!

B: 係呀，我都覺得呀！非常好！

B: 對啊！我同意！非常好！

37. Get some air - to go for a walk – 去唞唞氣，出去行一下

e.g.SC: 2 friends have been working on a project for some hours:

e.g.SC: 兩個朋友正在整緊個 project，都已經整咗幾粒鐘：

e.g.SC: 兩個朋友正在做一個 project，都已經做了幾個鐘頭：

A: I'm tired out! Let's go and get some air!

A: 我好鬼劫呀！我哋出去行下啦！

A: 我真是很累啊！我們出去行一下吧！

B: Yeah, I want to stretch my legs too. (Stretching legs has the same meaning as taking a walk)

B: 好喎！我都想出去伸下隻腳。（伸展隻腳係同出去行吓係同一個意思）

B: 好啊！我都想出去伸展一下。（伸展是和出去行一下是一樣意思）

55

e.g.SC: A mum has been indoors with her young children for a long time:

e.g.SC: 媽咪同啲女係屋企都有一段時間：

e.g.SC: 媽媽和女兒在家中已經很久了：

A (mum): Girls, let's go and get some air! Come on, put your shoes on!

A（媽媽）：呀女，出去行吓啦！快啲去著鞋啦！

A（媽媽）：女，出去行一下吧！快點去穿鞋子啦！

B: (girls): Yay!!

B:（女）：好呀！！

38. How one's doing for time? - does one have time, is one in a hurry – 你趕唔趕時間, 你趕不趕時間

e.g.SC: 2 friends have been chatting over a cup of coffee for an hour. A look at her watch and asks:

e.g.SC: 兩個朋友飲緊咖啡，傾緊計都成粒鐘。A 喺度望緊隻錶就問：

e.g.SC: 兩個朋友正在飲咖啡，傾談都有 1 小時。A 正在看錶子和問：

A: By the way, how're you doing for time?

A: 話時話，你係咪好趕時間呀？

A: 你是否很趕時間嗎？

B: Oh it's alright, I'm not in a hurry.

B: 吓，ok 喎。我唔趕時間。

B: 啊！OK！我不趕時間。

e.g.SC: In a meeting room, the manager has finished giving a presentation:

e.g.SC: 喺會議室，嗰經理啱啱講完個報告：

e.g.SC: 在會議室裏，經理剛剛說完了報告：

A: So that's it. How're we doing for time? Does anyone have any questions? We can have some Q & A now if you'd like.

A: 就係咁喇！我哋趕唔趕時間？有冇人有問題？如果你哋想嘅話，而家我哋可以做 Q & A。

A: 就是這樣吧！我們趕時間嗎？有沒有人有問題？如果你們想的話，現在我們可以做 Q & A。

That's it : it's the end, nothing more to follow. 就係咁多冇其他嘢啦，就是這樣沒有其他。

39. What's that all about? – when you don't understand why something is so popular, or the reason why it's there - 搞乜鬼野，搞咩，搞什麼鬼

e.g.SC: A dad has seen his teenage son's tattoo on his arm:

e.g.SC: 爹哋啱啱睇到佢個仔隻手臂有紋身：

e.g.SC: 爸爸剛剛看到兒子手臂有紋繪：

A (dad): Tom, I saw your tattoo that you've tried to hide from me, so what's that all about?

A（爹哋）：Tom，我見到你有個紋身，而且你收埋唔想我見到，你搞咩呀？

A（爸爸）：Tom，我看到你有一個紋繪，而且你不想我看見，你搞什麼鬼？

B: Sorry Dad, I didn't tell you. I just had one done.

B: Sorry 爹哋，我冇話俾你聽。我淨係整咗一個咋！

B: Sorry 爸爸，我沒有說給你聽。我只是有這一個吧！

e.g.SC: There's a queue right outside a shop:

e.g.SC: 喺間鋪頭出面，排緊隊：

e.g.SC: 在一間店外面，正在排隊：

A: What's this (the queue) all about?

A: 喂！搞咩呀！？出邊咁多人排隊嘅！

A: 喂！搞什麼鬼？！外面有很多人排隊啊！

B: No clue!

B: 唔知喎！

B: 不知道啊！

Queue (n), (v) (UK) 排隊 英式　**line** (US) 美式

40. Are you up for ___? (Q) - do you want to do this thing? - 你想唔想去做, 你想不想去做

e.g.SC: 2 friends chatting:

e.g.SC: 兩個朋友喺度傾緊計：

e.g.SC: 兩個朋友正在傾談中：

A: Hey Stewart, I haven't seen you for a long time, (are you) up for going to the cinema with me this Saturday?

A: 喂 Stewart，冇見你好耐啦喎，今個禮拜六想唔想去睇戲啊？

A: 喂 Stewart，很久沒有見面了，今個星期六想不想去看戲啊？

B: Yeah! I'm up for that!

B: 好呀，我都想去！

e.g.SC: 2 friends are near a pub (a British bar):

e.g.SC: 兩個朋友行緊一間英式酒吧：

e.g.SC: 兩個朋友正在行近英式酒吧：

A: Up for having a pint? It's 2 for 1 tonight! (have a pint = a pint of beer, around 500ml)

A: 想唔想要杯啤酒呀？今晚買二送一喎! (have a pint = a pint of 啤酒，大概 500 ml)

A: 想不想飲杯啤酒啊？我今晚買二送一啊！

Chapter 2

Idioms / phrasal verbs
俗語，成語

41. All over the place / shop – everywhere, disorganized - 亂晒籠 / 一塌糊塗

e.g.SC: 2 friends in a car, B is driving:

e.g.SC: 兩個朋友喺車度，B 揸緊車：

e.g.SC: 兩個朋友在車上，B 正在開車：

A: Look where you're going mate! You're all over the place – are you OK?

A: 喂！你睇住呀！你揸到亂晒籠喎！你冇嘢吖嘛？

A: 喂！你小心一點啊！你開車開到一塌糊塗啊！你沒有事嗎？

B: I'm fine! I've only had 2 glasses of wine!

B: 我得㗎喇！我淨係飲咗兩杯酒之嘛！

B: 我可以的！我只是喝了兩杯酒而已！

e.g.SC: A mum is talking to another mum on a side-line, watching their sons play soccer:

e.g.SC: 一個媽咪同緊另一個媽咪喺足球場度，睇緊佢哋啲仔踢緊波：

e.g.SC: 一個媽媽和另外一個媽媽在足球場上，看他們的兒子玩足球：

A: Oh – I've forgotten Oliver's shin pads! I'm all over the shop today – went to bed late last night and got up too early this morning!

A: 唉！我唔記得帶 Oliver 嘅護膝墊！我尋晚好夜先瞓，今朝有好早起身，所以今日亂晒籠！

A: 唉！我不記得帶 Oliver 的護脛墊啊！我昨晚很夜才睡，早上有很早起床，所以今天很一塌糊塗啊！

B: I know. I always try not to go out late on Saturday night because of the practice the next day. Why can't they have their training a little later in the day?

B: 係啦。我成日星期六晚唔出去㗎喇！因為第二日要去練習。點解佢哋 training 唔可以晏少少先開始嘅咩？

B: 對啊。我常常星期六晚上不出去的！因為星期天要去練習。為什麼他們訓練不可以晚一點才開始的嗎？

A: I know – so uncivilised!

A: 係啦！離晒譜㗎！

A: 對呀！太荒謬了！

Mate explained in this book.

uncivilised crazy, unreasonable - 瘋狂，不合理

42. At the end of the day – when everything else has been taken into consideration - 坐底 始終

e.g.SC: A and B talking about some problems that A has:

e.g.SC: A 同 B 傾緊 A 嘅問題：

e.g.SC: A 和 B 正在談 A 的問題：

A: I really don't know what to do! What do you think?

A: 唉！我真係唔知道點做好！你話呢？

A: 唉！我真是不知道怎樣做好！你說呢？

B: I think you should start looking for a job, but at the end of the day, you'll need to make your own decision.

B: 我就話你應該去搵份工先，但係始終你都要你自己去決定㗎喇。

B: 我就說你應該先去找工作吧！但是始終要你自己來決定的。

e.g.SC: A trying to console B:

e.g.SC: A 喺度安慰緊 B：

e.g.SC: A 正在安慰 B：

A: I know Andy is not so good to you, but at the end of the day, he's still your husband!

A: 雖然 Andy 對你唔係幾好，但係佢坐底始終都係你老公！

A: 雖然 Andy 對你不太好，但是他始終都是你老公！

B: I know.

B: 咁又係嘅。

B: 這倒是啊。

I know = you're right - 咁又係嘅 你是對的

43. Bang on about something (phr v)– to talk a lot about sth in a boring way - 猛咁講（好煩），囉唆 / 講不完（很煩）

e.g.SC: 2 university students talking about their professor's lecture:

e.g.SC: 兩個大學生講緊個教授嘅演講：

e.g.SC: 兩個大學生，正在談論教授的演講：

A: He kept banging on about his house hunting – nothing to do with the subject matter at all!

A: 佢猛咁講佢點樣去搵屋，完全都九唔搭八！

A: 佢講不完他怎樣去找屋子，他完全離了題！

B: I know – what a waste of time! Could have slept in a bit more this morning!

B: 係啦！嘥晒啲時間！早知我今朝就瞓多一陣先啦！

B: 是啊！浪費時間的！早知道早上就睡多一會吧！

e.g.SC: A husband and wife having an argument:

e.g.SC: 一對夫婦嘈緊交：

e.g.SC: 一對夫婦在爭吵中：

A: (wife): Why didn't you call when you knew you'd come home later? I got dinner prepared for you! You're always doing this!

A:（老婆）：你知道你會遲啲先返嚟，點解你唔打俾我呀？我已經煮咗你飯喇！你成日都係咁㗎喎！

A:（老婆）：你知道你會遲一些才回來，為什麼你不打電話給我我已經燒了你的飯啊！你常常都是這樣的！

B: Alright, alright, stop banging on about it!

B: 得喇！得喇！唔好咁囉唆啦！

B: 行！行！不要囉囉嗦嗦！

sleep in a bit more = sleep a bit longer 多睡一會兒

"You're always doing this!" 你成日都係咁㗎喎！你常常都是這樣的！ - implies the person has a habit of doing something.

We use the **present continuous tense** to express a **habit**.（習慣）

"You're **always** doing this!" – emphasis should be placed on '**always**' to express the annoyance at the frequency of the action performed. 語

氣係 'always' 加重表達次數，表達好煩　語氣在 'always' 加重表達次數，表達很煩

44. Chill out (phr v) – to calm down, relax - 冷靜啲，出去玩吓啦 / 冷靜一下，出去玩一下

e.g.SC: Two friends fighting, C says:

e.g.SC: 兩個朋友喺度打緊交，C 講:

e.g.SC: 兩個朋友在打交，C 說:

C: Chill out guys!

C: 喂！你哋冷靜啲啦！

C: 喂！你們冷靜一點吧！

e.g.SC: A calls B on a Saturday night:

e.g.SC: 星期六晚，A 打電話俾 B；

e.g.SC: 星期六晚上，A 打電話給 B：

A: Hey, I'm bored. Let's go and chill somewhere!

A: 喂！咁悶！出去玩吓啦！

A: 喂！很悶啊！出去玩一下吧！

B: Great! Where shall we go?

B: 好呀！去邊先？！

B: 好啊！去哪？

We can also use the word 'chill' on its own. 我們也可以單獨使用"chill"這個詞。

45. A close shave – very close to having an accident - 差啲就賴嘢 / 差一點就出事，很危險

e.g.SC: In the car, A driving:

e.g.SC: 喺車裏面，A 揸緊車：

e.g.SC: 在車裏面，A 正在開車：

A: I nearly had a prang here last time!

A: 嘩！我上次喺依度差啲出事呀！

A: 嘩！我上一次在這裏差一點就出事啊！

B: I had a couple of close shaves myself!

B: 我有幾次都差啲就賴嘢啦！

B: 我有多次都僥倖地脫險啊！

e.g.SC: A taking a bucket of water through to another room, when he/she nearly bumps into somebody:

e.g.SC: A 攞緊桶水去另一間房嘅時，就嚟撞到人：

e.g.SC: A 拿桶水去另外一間房間時，幾乎碰倒人：

A: Excuse me people, coming through!

A: 唔該借借！滾水呀！

A: 唔好意思呀！

B: (walk past accidentally) Oops! (A just avoids water spilling)

B: （咁啱行過）唉！（A 正在避開）

B: （剛剛行過）唉！（A 正在避開）

A: Close shave!

A: 嘩好險！差啲就賴嘢喇！

A: 嘩很危險！差一點就出事了！

"**Oops**!" is the sound you make when there's a small accident, or if you're trying to avoid an accident. 唉！

Also "**a close call**"- same meaning - **同樣的意思**

46. Crack someone up – to make sb laugh a lot - 搞笑 / 令人發大笑

e.g.SC: 2 good friends are chatting:

e.g.SC: 兩個好朋友傾緊計：

e.g.SC: 兩個好朋友正在聊天：

A: Samuel cracks me up all the time!

A: Samuel 成日搞我笑㗎！

A: Samuel 常常令我發大笑啊！

B: I know! He's hilarious!

B: 係啦！佢好好笑㗎！

B: 是啊！他很滑稽啊！

e.g.SC: 2 friends talking about C:

e.g.SC: 兩個朋友講緊 C：

e.g.SC: 兩個朋友在說關於 C：

A: Randy is so funny! His jokes crack me up every time!

A: 呀 Randy 真係超好笑㗎！佢啲笑話成日都笑爆我！

A: Randy 真是很好笑的！他的笑話常常都讓我，笑死！

B: Hard to keep a straight face when he's around, that's for sure!

B: 講真，好難對住佢唔笑囉！

B: 真的，當他在的時候，很難不笑啊！

Chatting explained in this book

Hilarious very funny

To keep a straight face – to not laugh 唔笑 不笑

Funny (adj) – making people laugh, hilarious 好笑

BUT **Funny (adj)** – strange 古怪

e.g. a **funny** (hilarious) book

BUT a **funny** (strange) person

e.g. 一本好笑嘅書 e.g.一個古怪嘅人

Fun (n/adj) – n – to have fun = to have enjoyment 開心 暢快

e.g. We **had** a lot of fun at Ocean Park last week.

e.g. 我哋上個禮拜喺海洋公園玩得好開心呀。我們上個星期在海洋公園玩得很暢快。

- **adj** – enjoyable 玩得開心 玩得愉快

e.g. Have a **fun** weekend!

e.g. 週末玩得開心啲啦！有一個愉快的，週末吧！

That's for sure = definitely, we're sure about this point. 好肯定嘅 肯定的

e.g. We don't know much about Cindy, but she's a good person **that's for sure**.

e.g. 我哋唔係好識 Cindy，不過有樣嘢好肯定嘅就係佢好好人。我跟 Cindy 不太熟悉，不過肯定她是個好人。

47. Crack on (phr v) – to continue - 繼續

e.g.SC: 2 friends resting from a walk in the mountains:

e.g.SC: 兩個朋友行山，喺度休息緊：

e.g.SC: 兩個朋友登山，正在休息中：

A: It's getting dark – looks like rain!

A: 嘩！嗰天越嚟越黑喎！好似想落雨！

A: 嘩！天越來越黑啊！好像要下雨！

B: Let's crack on before it chucks it.

B: 趁佢未落雨，我哋繼續行啦！

B: 還未下雨，我們繼續行吧！

e.g.SC: 2 students writing up their work:

e.g.SC: 兩個學生一齊做緊功課：

e.g.SC: 兩個學生一起做功課：

A: Did you see 'The Funny Show' on Pearl last night? It was hilarious!

A: 喂！你尋晚有冇睇明珠台嗰 'The Funny Show' 呀？真係超搞笑！

A: 喂！你昨晚有沒有看了明珠台的 'The Funny Show' 嗎？真是很好笑啊！

B: Yes, I saw it - really good show! By the way, let's crack on or we'll never get it done today!

B: 我有睇，係好好睇呀。喂！我哋繼續做啦！如果唔係今日我哋做唔晒㗎喇！

B: 我有看啊，是很好看的。喂！我們繼續做吧！不然今天我們做不完了！

looks like rain = looks like it's going to rain - 就像要下雨一樣

chucks it - rains heavily - 大雨

Crack on **+ with** (prep) sth

48. Crank it up (phr v)– to increase - 加重啲，加大啲 / 加重一些，加大一些

e.g.SC: 2 friends listening to music:

e.g.SC: 兩個朋友聽緊音樂：

e.g.SC: 兩個朋友正在聽音樂：

A: Hey, this is my fav – crank it up!

A: 喂！呢隻我至愛呀！大聲啲啦！

A: 喂！這首歌是我的最愛啊！大聲一點吧！

B: Ok!

B: 哦！

B: 好！

e.g.SC: 2 brothers sitting in a living room with indoor heating on:

e.g.SC: 兩個兄弟坐喺廳度，開緊暖爐：

e.g.SC: 兩個兄弟坐在廳中開暖爐：

A: Can you crank up the heating? It's freezing here!

A: 喂！你可唔可以開大啲個暖爐呀？依度好鬼死凍呀！

A: 喂！你可不可以開大一點暖爐啊？這裏冷死人！

B: (playing computer games): Why can't you do it? I'm busy killing the aliens right now!

B: （玩緊電腦 game）你去開啦！我而家忙緊打外星人呀！

B: 你去開啦！我現在忙着打外星人啊！

fav= favorite - 最愛

49. A dead loss – sb / sth useless - 好屎，嘥氣啦 / 沒用的，浪費時間的

e.g.SC: A and B are having a row, C said to A:

e.g.SC: A 同 B 嘈緊交，C 同 A 講：

e.g.SC: A 和 B 吵架，C 跟 A 說：

C: Alan, stop fighting with Steve – it's a dead loss.

C: 喂 Alan！唔好再同 Steve 嘈啦！講多都嘥氣啦！

C: 喂 Alan！不要再和 Steve 吵啦！多說都浪費時間吧！

e.g.SC: At the office, supervisor A says to manager B:

e.g.SC: 喺 office 度，A 主任同 B 經理講：

e.g.SC: 在 office 內，A 主任更 B 經理說：

A: I think Edward may be a very talented accountant, but as a manager for his team, he's a dead loss!

A: 經理！我諗 Edward 係一個非常好嘅會計師，但係佢做 team manager 黎講呢就真係好屎喇！

A: 經理！我覺得 Edward 是一個非常好的會計師，但是當團隊經理他就真是很窩囊啦！

50. Dive in (phr v)– to jump into doing sth eagerly - 好心急咁樣去做啲嘢 / 急不及待

e.g.SC: At a restaurant. The food has arrived:

e.g.SC: 喺餐廳度，啲嘢食到咗：

e.g.SC: 在餐廳內：食物到了：

A: Hey guys – let's dive in!

A: 喂！食嘢喇！

A: 喂！吃東西吧！

B: Yippee!

B: 好嘢！

B: 好啊！

e.g.SC: At home, a father is talking to his son:

e.g.SC: 喺屋企，爸爸同緊嗰仔講：

e.g.SC: 在家裏，爸爸跟兒子說：

A: Son, you just can't dive into anything without thinking about the consequences!

A: 仔！做嘢唔好咁冇耐性，要諗清楚嗰後果先呀！

A: 兒子！做事情別沒有耐性，先要想清楚後果才對啊！

B: Dad – I know!

B: 我知喇！老竇！

B: 我知道啊！爸爸！

To Dive (v) = to drop - 減低

e.g. Production **dived** = production was reduced. 生產減低

take a dive = suddenly get worse. e.g. Business **took a dive** last year. e.g. 舊年生意差咗。去年生意差了。

51. Fair enough – ok, reasonable, understandable - 有道理，係嘅 / 對啊

e.g.SC: In a class meeting:

e.g.SC: 喺課室會議度：

e.g.SC: 課室會議中：

A: We've overspent by $100 after buying a present for Mr Morris!

A: Mr Morris 份禮物，我哋已經超出咗$100 喫喇！

A: 陳先生的禮物，我們已經超出了一百塊錢啊！

B: But the money came from the charity sale anyway. So it wasn't exactly our money.

B: 但其實啲錢係捐款而黎，又唔係我哋啲錢。

B: 但是其實錢是捐款回來的，又不是我們的錢。

A: Fair enough, but it was still not budgeted for.

A: 係嘅！但係依個唔係預算之內喎！

A: 對啊！但是這個不是預算之內啊！

e.g.SC: 2 kids fighting over a toy:

e.g.SC: 兩個細路爭嘢玩：

e.g.SC: 兩個小孩因為玩具爭吵：

A: Mum, he took away my model car! It's mine!

A: 媽咪！佢攞咗我間模型車呀！係我㗎！

A: 媽媽！她拿了我的模型車啊！是我的！

B: Your brother's only borrowing it from you. Please let him play with it for a little while.

B: 細佬借嚟玩吓啫！你俾佢玩一陣啦！

B: 弟弟借來玩一下！你給他玩一會兒吧！

A: But it's mine! He shouldn't have taken it without asking!

A: 架車係我㗎！佢唔應該冇問過我就攞咗去㗎嘛！

A: 這架車是我的！他不應該沒有問過我就拿去了！

B: Fair enough, (turning to brother) Eric, do ask your brother first next time.

B: 咁又係嘅！（轉身向着細佬）Eric 呀！你下次要問咗哥哥先呀！

B: 對啊！（轉身向弟弟）Eric！你下次要問了哥哥才拿啊！

To borrow (**from**) 人借俾你 別人借給你 BUT lend (**to**) 你借俾人 你借給別人

e.g. A: Can I borrow $200 from you please? NOT Can you borrow me $200?

e.g. A: 你可唔可以借兩舊水嚟呀？你可不可以借兩百塊錢給我？

B: Yeah OK. I'll lend it to you, but you must pay me back next week!

B: OK。我會借俾你，不過下個星期你要還返俾我㗎!

B: OK。我會借給你，不過下星期你要還給我啊！

52. Fingers crossed – to hope for the best - 希望，希望好運啦

e.g.SC: At an examination hall:

e.g.SC: 喺考試場度：

e.g.SC: 考試場內：

A: Hope the paper's not too hard!

A: 希望啲試卷唔會好難啦！

A: 希望試卷不會太難！

B: Finger crossed!

B: 希望啦！

B: 希望好運吧！

e.g.SC: 2 friends talking about the weather:

e.g.SC: 兩個朋友講緊天氣：

e.g.SC: 兩個朋友正在說關於天氣：

A: Hope it won't rain tomorrow or the outing will be cancelled!

A: 希望聽日唔好落雨啦，如果唔係個活動就會 cancel 㗎喇！

A: 希望明天不會下雨吧，如果不是這個活動就會取消了！

B: Finger crossed!

B: 希望啦！

B: 希望吧！

The paper here refers to the question/exam paper. A paper can also means a newspaper.

e.g. A: Can you fetch me the paper (報紙) please?

e.g. A: 你可唔可以攞張報紙過嚟呀唔該？可以拿報紙給我嗎？

B: Sure.

B: 哦。好啊。

An **outing** = an activity that happens outdoors. It can be anything from going to the beach, to hiking in the mountains. 戶外活動

'**Out**' can be a pre-fix e.g. **out**side, **out**do, **out**doors. These words have the meaning of "out" 外 to them.

53. Fire away (U.K.) / Shoot (US) to say - 講呀

e.g.SC: 2 friends on the phone:

e.g.SC: 兩個朋友傾緊電話：

e.g.SC: 兩個朋友正在電話談話中：

A: Here's Amanda's number – have you pen and paper?

A: 嗱！呢個係 Amanda 嘅電話 number，你有冇紙同筆？

A: 嗱！這個是 Amanda 的電話號碼，你有沒有紙和筆？

B: Yup. Fire away!

B: 有！**講呀**！

B: 有！講吧！

A: It's 263-6578

A: 263-6578

e.g.SC: After a sales talk:

e.g.SC: 銷售講座完後：

e.g.SC: 銷售講座完後：

A: (salesman): …I think that's it. Any questions?

A:（售貨員）：…我諗差唔多喇，有冇咩問題？

A: …我想差不多吧，有沒有什麼問題？

B: Yes – I've got a question.

B: 有，我有嚼問題。

B: 有，我有一個問題。

A: Fire away!

A: 講呀！

A: 講吧！

yup = yes

80

54. Go haywire – out of control - 癲晒，亂晒籠 / 失去控制，混亂

e.g.SC: At the party:

e.g.SC: 喺 party 度：

e.g.SC: 在 party 裏：

A: Things are going haywire in here. Think we'd better call it a day!

A: 嘩！成班人都玩到癲晒。不如我哋散 band 啦！

A: 嘩！這班人都玩到失去控制。我們完吧！

B: Ok. Let's tell them to go home.

B: OK。咁叫佢哋返屋企啦！

B: OK。叫他們回家吧！

e.g.SC: On the phone. A speaking to B:

e.g.SC: A 同 B 傾緊電話，A 話：

e.g.SC: A 和 B 正在談電話，A 說：

A: What's up with you lately?

A: 你最近點呀？

A: 你近來怎麼樣啊？

B: Things are going haywire at the moment – so, no, not so good.

B: 呢排做嘢做到我亂晒籠！唔係幾好囉！

B: 我近來我的事情很混亂！不是很好啊！

call it a day = end it 完

55. Go out with somebody – to have a date with sb, to have a relationship with sb - 拍拖

e.g.SC: 2 good friends are chatting:

e.g.SC: 兩個好朋友傾緊計：

e.g.SC: 兩個好朋友正在聊天：

A: Hey, are you going out with Vicky at the moment? She seems nice!

A: 喂！你而家係唔係同緊 Vicky 拍拖啫？你同佢好似好啱 key 喎！

A: 喂！你現在是不是跟 Vicky 拍拖啊？你和她好像很合得來啊！

B: No, we're just friends! – Well, maybe good friends.

B: 唔係呀！我哋只係朋友嚟咋！嗯，可能係好朋友囉！

B: 不是啊！我們只是朋友而已！嗯，可能是好朋友吧！

e.g.SC: A mum is talking to her daughter:

e.g.SC: 媽咪同緊嗰女講：

e.g.SC: 媽媽跟女兒說：

A: (mum): Carmen, you've been going out with Ricky for a long time now. Any plans to tie the knot?

A:（媽咪）：Carmen，你同 Ricky 都行咗好耐喇喎！有冇諗住結婚啫？

A: Carmen，你話 Ricky 都一起很久了！有沒有想過結婚啊？

B: (daughter): Mum! Give me a break! I'll know when it's time!

B:（女）：媽咪！唔該你啦！我會知幾時先係啱時候㗎喇！

B:（女）：媽！別要這樣吧！我會知道何時才是好的時候的啊！

Give me a break explained in this book

To tie the knot = to marry 結婚

hang out with sb = **spend time with sb**. Can be shortened to **'hang'**. hea 下 坐一下

e.g. 我諗我會去家姐屋企 hea 下囉。我想我會去姐姐的家坐一下吧。

56. Go with the flow (idiom)– let the event / situation develop naturally - 順其自然

e.g.SC: 2 housewives talking:

e.g.SC: 兩個太太傾緊計：

e.g.SC: 兩個太太在聊天：

A: You've been married for a while now – any plans for a family soon?

A: 喂！你同你老公結咗婚咁耐，其實有冇打算生過 BB 呀？

A: 喂！你和你老公結了婚那麼久，其實有沒有打算生孩子啊？

B: Well, we'll just go with the flow.

B: 嗯……順其自然啦！

B: 嗯……順其自然吧！

e.g.SC: 2 colleagues talking about a training course:

e.g.SC: 兩個同事講緊嗰訓練課程：

e.g.SC: 兩個同事再談一個訓練課程：

A: The trainer asked us to prepare an activity for today's session. Did you do it?

A: 教練叫我哋今日準備一個活動喎！你做咗未呀？

A: 教練叫我們今天準備一個活動。你做了沒有啊？

B: No, I'll just go with the flow!

B: 冇喎！順其自然啦！

B: 還沒有啊！順其自然吧！

play it by ear (idiom) -similar meaning 見機行事

84

57. A good / bad call – a good/bad decision - 好 / 壞嘅決定，好在，蠢咗 / 好 / 壞的決定，蠢了

e.g.SC: 2 ladies cooking:

e.g.SC: 兩個女人煮緊嘢食：

e.g.SC: 兩個女人烹調食物中：

A: Look at the beef joint – it's beautiful! Good call to put foil on top before popping it into the oven.

A: 嘩！你睇吓件牛骨幾靚吖！好在用錫紙包住先放入焗爐。

A: 嘩！你看看這件牛骨很美啊！幸好用錫紙包起來，然後才放進焗爐裏。

B: Yeah! My mum taught me the trick!

B: 係呀！我媽咪教我依一招㗎！

B: 對啊！我媽媽教我這一套的！

e.g.SC: Some friends trying to leave a stadium after a music concert:

e.g.SC: 嗰 concert 完咗，一班朋友正在離開緊：

e.g.SC: 音樂會完了，一班朋友正在離開中：

A: Bad call to leave along with the crowd! Now look at the taxi queue!

A: 蠢咗㗎！咁多人一齊走！你睇吓條的士龍尾！

A: 蠢了！那麼多人一起走！你看看的士已經排成了長隊！

B: Oh dear! Let's just take the tube then!

B: 哎呀！咁不如去搭地鐵啦！

B: 哎喲！去坐地鐵吧！

Popping explained in this book.

Foil = aluminium foil for baking or roasting 錫紙

Cling film = the plastic that one puts on food to keep it fresh 保鮮紙

Joint of beef 牛骨 – the cut of beef that's usually for roasting in the oven.

Minced beef 免治牛肉 and **beef fillets** 牛柳 are more for frying and baking.

58. Have a lot of / no time for something / somebody – like/not like or interested/not interested in sth/sb - 鍾意，唔鍾意, li-ke, 唔 li-ke / 喜歡，不喜歡

e.g.SC: In the student canteen:

e.g.SC: 喺學校 canteen 度：

e.g.SC: 在學校食堂：

A: Hey Cathy – I heard you've got Mrs Leeton as your tutor!

A: 喂 Cathy！聽人講 Mrs Leeton 呢做你 tutor 喎！

A: 喂 Cathy！聽說 Leeton 老師當你的導師啊！

B: I know. She's great! patient and knowledgeable – have a lot of time for her.

B: 係呀！佢超好㗎！又有耐性，又有知識！我都好 li-ke 佢㗎！

B: 對啊！她很好喎！幾有耐性，又有知識！我也很喜歡她的！

e.g.SC: At the office:

e.g.SC: 喺 office 度：

e.g.SC: 在 office ：

A: Hey, it's Mark 6 day today – did you buy any?

A: 喂！今日開六合彩喎！你有冇買呀？

A: 喂！今天開六合彩啊！你買了沒有？

B: I've got no time for this sort of thing. There's no free lunch!

B: 我唔鍾意依啲嘢嘅！邊度有免費午餐食㗎！

B: 我不喜歡這些東西！哪裏有免費午餐呢！

A: There's nothing wrong with trying your luck!

A: 冇嘢㗎，試吓運氣之嘛！

A: 沒有什麼的，試試運氣而已！

There's no free lunch = There's no reward without hard work - 沒有努力就沒有回報

To try + v +ing + sth.

e.g. "Try lifting these weights". e.g. 你試吓舉依啲啞鈴。你是舉這些啞鈴。

Let me have a try/have a go = let me try 等我試吓。給我試一下。But **NOT** Do a try.

Try sb 問吓 使問 = try to ask sb (as in the SC below)

59. Have too much on someone's plate (idiom) – too occupied, busy - 太多嘢做 / 太多事情要做

e.g.SC: A lady wants to ask her friend to help to organize a birthday do.

e.g.SC: A 女士想去問吓佢朋友幫手搞嗰生日 party：

e.g.SC: A 女士想問一下她朋友幫她弄一個生日派對：

A: Helena, do you think you can organize this birthday do for Alex?

A: Helena，你諗你可唔可以幫 Alex 搞嗰生日 party 呀？

A: Helena，你想你可不可以幫 Alex 弄一個生日派對呢？

B: Sorry, I have got too much on my plate lately. Try Ross.

B: 唔好意思喇！最近我好忙呀！不如問吓 Ross 啦！

B: 不好意思！近來我很忙啊！問一下 Ross 吧！

e.g.SC: A husband and a wife talking:

e.g.SC: 兩公婆傾緊計：

e.g.SC: 兩夫婦正在聊天：

A: (wife): Darling, you can't take this on – you've got too much on your plate at the moment!

A:（老婆）：老公，你可以再接嘢做㗎喇！你而家已經有好多嘢做喇！

A:（老婆）：老公，你不可以再拿東西來做了！你現在已經有很多事情要做啊！

B: (husband): I know sweetheart. But he's my boss! – I can't say no.

B:（老公）：我知，老婆！但係佢係我老細，我唔可以話唔得囉。

B:（老公）：我知道，老婆！但是他是我老闆，我不可以說不做的吧。

60. It's a long shot – sth that is difficult to do - 都幾難喎

e.g.SC: 2 friends talking about the job that B has applied for:

e.g.SC: 兩個朋友講緊 B 去見份工：

e.g.SC: 兩個朋友在說 B 去面試的事情：

A: So do you think you can get the job then?

A: 咁你諗你會唔會見成份工呢？

A: 你覺得你求職能成功嗎？

B: It's a long shot! There were hundreds of applicants!!

B: 都幾難喇！嗰度成百個人去申請呀！！

B: 很難吧！哪裏有超過一百個申請人啊！！

e.g.SC: A rugby team playing against a strong team. The team captain talks to the team members:

e.g.SC: 一對欖球隊要對住班強隊。隊長同啲隊員講：

e.g.SC: 一對欖球隊要對強隊。隊長跟隊員說：

A: (Team Captain): It's a long shot winning the Tigers this time, but we'll give it a good go!!

A:（隊長）：今次都幾難去贏 Tiger，不過我哋會盡晒力嘅！！

A:（隊長）：這次都幾難去贏 Tiger 隊，不過我們會盡全力的！

B: (all): Yes, Captain!

B:（全部人）：係呀隊長！

B:（全部人）：是啊，隊長！

It's a tall order - similar meaning 都幾難喎

61. Lose the plot (idiom)– cannot understand/deal with what is happening, confused - 唔明白，九唔搭八 / 不明白

e.g.SC: 2 English–speaking people have just got into a taxi in Hong Kong:

e.g.SC: 兩個外國人喺香港，啱啱上咗部的士：

e.g.SC: 兩個外國人在香港，剛剛上了計程車：

A: Peng yau! We want to go to the British Embassy please. How much is the ride going to be?

A: 朋友，我哋想去英國大使館。搭過去要幾多錢呀？

A: 朋友，我們想去英國大使館。到那裏要多少錢呢？

B: (Chinese taxi driver): Yeah British! Difficult people! UK – weather no good…

B:（的士司機）：係呀英國佬大晒咩？嗰度天氣又唔好……

B:（的士司機）：對啊英國人真混帳，那裏天氣有不好……

A: (Talking to C): Think he's lost the plot. You try!

A:（同緊 C 講）：睇佢九唔搭八咁款！你試吓啦！

A:（在跟 C 說）：看來他都不明白啊！你試一試吧！

C: Peng yau! Embassy? Money??

C: 朋友 - 大使館？錢？？

e.g.SC: At a bank: a couple asking for some information:

e.g.SC: 喺銀行，兩公婆問緊一啲資料：

e.g.SC: 在銀行裏，一對夫婦正在問一些資料：

A: (husband): Just want to know what kinds of savings plans you have.

A:（老公）：只係想知道你哋有邊幾個存款計劃。

A:（老公）：只是想知道你們有什麼存款計劃。

B: (bank staff): Oh, we have the basic plan, the star plan, and the galaxy plan. The basic plan has the following…… (2 minutes later). We also have 5 kinds of house content insurance plans…

B:（銀行職員）：啊，我哋有個人存款，星級存款，同埋特級存款。咁個人存款就有以下…（2分鐘之後）我哋仲有五種嘅房屋保險計劃……

B:（銀行職員）：啊，我們有個人存款，星級存款和特級存款。個人存款就有以下…（2分鐘之後）我們還有五種的房屋保險計劃……

A: (whispering to wife): Think she's lost the plot. Let's get out of here!!

A:（細細聲同老婆講）：佢九唔搭八喎！快啲走啦！

A:（少少聲，跟老婆說）：她在胡說八道，啊！我們快走吧！

A **taxi** 的士= a **cab**.

A taxi driver 的士佬 的士司機= a cabbie

A (the cabbie): I've lost the way!

A（的士佬）：我蕩失咗路呀！我迷了路啊！

B: What! You're a cabbie and you've lost the way?

B: 喂！你係的士佬喎，又唔會蕩失路嘅？喂！你是的士司機，又怎麼會迷路呢？

62. Mess around / faff / goof / muck around (phr v) – to play around, not serious - 搞搞震，玩玩吓 / 胡鬧

e.g.SC: A boss is telling off his subordinates:

e.g.SC: 老闆鬧緊下屬：

e.g.SC: 老闆正在罵下屬：

A: Hey you guys! Stop mucking about! – get on with the work!

A: 喂！唔好再喺度搞搞震喇！快啲出去做嘢啦！

A: 喂！不好在唔鬧了！快去做事吧！

B: Right!

B: 哦！

B: 哦！

e.g.SC: 2 students are in school detention. They're supposed to be working:

e.g.SC: 兩個學生留緊堂，佢哋應該做緊功課：

e.g.SC: 兩個學生留校，他們應該在做功課中：

A: …. give the pen back!

A: ……俾返支筆我呀！

A: ……那筆還給我啊!

B: … there!

B: ……嗱!

B: ……給!

C: (teacher walks over): You two – stop faffing around! Get on with the work!

C: (先生行過嚟): 你兩個唔好搞搞震喇!快啲做嘢啦!

C: (先生行過來): 你兩個不好,再胡鬧!快去做功課吧!

Mess + prep (about/around) 玩玩吓 胡鬧

Mess about + with sth – to play with it annoyingly. 玩爛

e.g. The children **messed about** with the camcorder and broke it.

e.g. 啲細路玩完部攝影機仲整爛咗。小孩玩這部攝影機,弄破了。

BUT **Mess about + with** sb – to be in a casual relationship with sb. 同人嘅關係,玩玩吓 偷情

e.g. Alan has been messing about with his secretary for a long time = Alan has not been in a serious relationship with his secretary for a long time.

e.g. Alan 同佢秘書,玩玩吓都一段時間 Alan 和他的秘書偷情好一段時間了

Idiot = a stupid person 蠢材 傻子

63. Off the top of somebody's head (idiom)– just guessing or using memory, without thinking hard - 就咁諗 / 就這樣想

e.g.SC: 2 friends trying to take some money out from the cash machine:

e.g.SC: 兩個朋友喺 ATM 度，等緊攞錢：

e.g.SC: 兩個朋友在 ATM ，等提款：

A: Hey, what are you waiting for?

A: 喂！你做咩企喺度唔撳錢呀？

A: 喂！你做什麼呆了不題款啊？

B: Oh dear! Can't remember my pin off the top of my head! It's a new card, you see…

B: 哎呀！我突然間諗唔到嗰密碼呀！依張新卡嚟㗎……

B: 哎呀！我突然間想不到密碼啊！這張是新信用卡……

e.g.SC: 2 students talking about their assignment:

e.g.SC: 兩個同學講緊佢哋啲功課：

e.g.SC: 兩個同學正在談他們的功課：

A: Do you remember what Mr. Lee said about how many marks this assignment is out of the total?

A: 喂，你記唔記得 Mr. Lee 講個關於依個 assignment 佔幾多分？

A: 喂，你記唔記得李先生這個習作佔多少分？

B: Off the top of my head – think it's 30 out of 100? – not very sure… we'd better check!

B: 就咁諗好似係 100 分佔 30 分？不過唔係咁肯定！我哋最好 check 吓先！

B: 就這樣，想好像是 100 分佔 30 分？不過不是太肯定！我們最好問一下吧！

To **wait + prep (for),** BUT **await + no prep**. They mean the same thing but await is more formal – more for written English.

e.g. At the end of a letter, we write**: I await a reply from you**. e.g. 喺信嘅尾部，我哋寫：我等你嘅回覆。稍後回覆

64. On the trot – one after another, continuously – 連續 / 不停地

e.g.SC: Two good friends on the phone:

e.g.SC: 兩個好朋友，傾緊電話：

e.g.SC: 兩個好朋友正在談電話：

A: I've been revising for the exams for several days on the trot! I'm absolutely knackered!

A: 嘩！我依幾晚連續開夜車，都係為咗啲考試，超劫呀！

A: 嘩！我這幾晚不停地溫習得很晚都是為了這個考試，好累啊！

B: You'd better take a good rest when they finish then!

B: 咁你一考完試，就好好去休息吓啦！

B: 那你考試完了，就好好去休息一下吧！

e.g.SC: At an inter-school swimming gala:

e.g.SC: 喺校際游泳會度：

e.g.SC: 在校際游泳會中：

A: How is our school team doing?

A: 我哋嘅校隊點呀？

A: 我們的校隊怎麼樣啊？

B: We've been winning 3 races on the trot!

B: 我哋已經連續贏咗三次比賽喇！

B: 我們已經連續贏了三次比賽了！

knackered explained in this book

65. Pull it off (phr v)– succeed in doing sth difficult - 做得到

e.g.SC: A secretary is wearing a mini-skirt to work:

e.g.SC: 嗰秘書着緊條短裙仔返工：

e.g.SC: 秘書穿着一條短裙子上班：

A: Did you see what Susan's wearing today? A mini-skirt! Would you say she's 50-odd years old?

A: 喂！你睇唔睇到 Susan 今日着咗咩呀？短裙仔呀！佢有冇成 50 幾歲呀？

A: 喂！你看不看到 Susan 今天穿什麼啊？短裙子啊！她有沒有 50 多歲了？

B: Yes, she's 53! But why not if she can still pull it off?!

B: 有，佢 53 喇！但係佢着得起喎！

B: 有，她 53 了！但是她穿得不錯啊！

e.g.SC: At a children's Christmas party:

e.g.SC: 喺兒童聖誕 party 度：

e.g.SC: 在兒童聖誕 party 裏：

A: Who's Santa Claus? Surely it's not Johnny's dad, is it?

A: 邊個做聖誕老人呀？唔係 Johnny 個老竇吖嘛？

A: 誰當聖誕老人？不是 Johnny 的爸爸嗎？

B: It sure is! Only he can pull it off with that belly of his!!

B: 梗係佢啦！佢有嗰大肚傻子，淨係佢先至做得到㗎咋！！

B: 一定是他啦！他有這麼大的肚子，只是他才能做得到啊！！

50 odd years old – someone in their 50s. (51-59 years old) 50 幾歲

In the 50's – in the 1950s (1951-1959) 50 年代

e.g. House prices were much cheaper in the 50s. e.g. 50 年代樓價比而家平好多。50 年代的樓價比現在便宜很多。

Belly = stomach 肚

66. Put foot in it – to be involved in sth - 干涉，架樑，洗濕咗頭 / 牽涉

e.g.SC: 2 people arguing. B tries to stop them:

e.g.SC: 兩個人嘈緊交，B 嘗試停止佢哋：

e.g.SC: 兩個人爭吵中，B 嘗試停止他們：

A: You're being unreasonable! I won't have it!

A: 你都完全唔講道理嘅！我點都唔會接受囉！

A: 你都完全不講道理的！我都不會接受！

B: I don't mean to put my foot in it, but you two should just hear each other out first!

B: 我唔係想做架樑，但係你哋兩個應該要聽咗對方點講先啦！

B: 我不是想牽涉，但是你們兩個應該先聽了對方怎樣說的！

e.g.SC: 2 university friends talking about a project they have to do:

e.g.SC: 兩個大學朋友講緊佢哋要做個 project：

e.g.SC: 兩個大學朋友正在講他們要做的計劃：

A: Jordan, how come you're in our group?

A: 喂 Jordan，點解你會喺我哋個 group 度嘅？

A: 喂 Jordan，為什麼你會在我們這個組裏邊的？

B: I know. Professor Ng told me to join you after I'd asked him a couple of questions about this topic you're doing. I've put my foot in it now – couldn't say no to him. So, here I am!

B: 係啦。我去問咗吳教授兩個關於你而家做緊嗰個 topic 嘅問題之後，佢叫我哋 join 你哋嘅。我已經洗濕咗個頭喇 而家唔可以向佢 say no㗎喇！所以我咪喺度囉！

B: 是啊。我問了吳教授兩個關於你現在做那個題目的問題之後，他叫我加入你們的。我已經牽涉了。現在不可以向他說不啊！所以我在這裏啊！

Have it = accept 接受

To hear sb out – to spend time listening to sb's point of view or explanation 聽對方講 聽對方怎樣說

how come = why 點解,為什麼

A couple + of – two, or a few 兩，幾個

100

e.g. I've only been waiting for a couple of minutes. = a few minutes, more than 2.

e.g. 我不過等咗幾分鐘啫。我都是等了幾分鐘的吧。

A couple (n) – a pair of people, usually a man and a woman together. 一對男女

Nowadays it could be 2 men or 2 women. （現代講法）一對男人，一對女人

67. Ring a bell (idiom)– familiar, to be reminded of - 好熟，有印象 / 熟悉

e.g.SC: At a student reunion camp, A talking to B:

e.g.SC: 喺學生聚會營度，A 同緊 B 講：

e.g.SC: 在學生聚會營裏，A 跟 B 說：

A: Your name rings a bell. Did you go to "Tang's Primary School?"

A: 吖！你個名好熟，你有冇喺'鄧記小學'度讀書？

A: 你的名字好熟悉，你有沒有在'鄧記小學'裏上過學？

B: No, I think you have the wrong person. I never went to that school.

B: 冇呀！我諗你認錯人喇！我都冇喺嗰間學校讀過。

B: 沒有啊！我想你錯了！我從來沒有在這間學校上過學。

e.g.SC: At a property agency. Agent B talking to client A:

e.g.SC: 喺地產公司度，B 經紀同緊 A 客人講：

e.g.SC: 在地產公司裏，B 經紀跟 A 客人說：

A: Want to look at houses in the Elton area? Does this town ring any bells?

A: 想去睇吓 Elton 嗰邊啲屋。嗰頭有冇印象呀？

A: 想去看一下 Elton 那邊的屋子。那邊有沒有印象嗎？

B: Yes, I've shown clients houses in that area before. I'll get a list and show you some houses tomorrow.

B: 有，我之前有帶過啲客去嗰度睇屋。我聽日攞埋張 list 同你去睇屋啦。

B: 有，我以前有帶過一些客人去那邊看房子。我明天拿那張清單跟你去看房子吧。

68. Rip off (phr v) – to get someone to pay more than they need to - 搵笨 / 欺騙

e.g.SC: At a shopping centre -

e.g.SC: 喺商場度：

e.g.SC: 在商場：

A: How much did you pay for that vase?

A: 依個花樽，你買咗幾多錢呀？

A: 這個花瓶你買了多少錢啊？

B: £500! What a bargain! It's made of crystal!

B: 500磅囉！超抵呀！水晶做㗎！

B: 500磅啊！很便宜啊！用水晶做的！

A: Karen, you've been ripped off! This isn't crystal – it's glass!

A: Karen，你俾人搵咗笨喇！依個唔係水晶，係玻璃嚟㗎！

A: Karen，你想當了！這個不是水晶，是玻璃啊！

B: B has a friend who's visiting:

B: B 嘅朋友嚟咗探佢：

B: B 的朋友來了探望她：

A: So where are you taking me today? The Ladies Market in Mong Kok?

A: 咁你今日帶我去邊度呀？旺角嗰條女人街？

A: 你今天帶我去哪裏？旺角那條女人街？

B: No, they always rip tourists off there! I'll take you somewhere else for shopping. How about Sheung Wan? There are some interesting shops there.

B: 唔係呀！嗰度啲人成日搵啲遊客笨㗎！我會帶你去另一個地方 shopping。不如去上環啦！嗰度有啲幾得意嘅嘢買㗎！

B: 不是喔！那裏的人常常欺騙遊客啊！我會帶你去另一個地方買東西。我們去上環吧！哪裏有一些很有趣的東西買的！

<u>A bargain</u> (n) – something very cheap 超抵 很便宜

69. Screw something up / mess up / botch up / cock up (phr v) – to do sth badly - 搞禍咗，攪喝晒 / 弄得很差

e.g.SC: A has just come back from the hairdresser's:

e.g.SC: A 啱啱喺髮型屋度返嚟：

e.g.SC: A 剛剛從理髮店回來：

A: Look at my hair! The hairdresser has really botched it up this time!

A: 嘩！睇吓我啲頭髮！！嗰髮型師，今次真係搞禍咗我啲頭髮呀！

A: 嘩！看一下我的頭髮！！這個理髮師，今次真的把我的頭髮弄得很差啊！

B: Oh my god! Worse than any bad hair days I've seen you have!

B: 哎喲！前所未見個咁樣衰嘅髮型囉！

B: 哎喲！前所未見過這樣差的髮型啊！

e.g.SC: B has just come back from a long-haul flight from the UK. He's on the phone with his friend:

e.g.SC: B 啱啱喺英國坐完長途機返嚟。佢同緊佢嘅朋友傾緊電話：

e.g.SC: B 剛剛從英國坐完長途機回來。他和他的朋友正在電話談話中：

A: So how was the trip?

A: 喂！旅行好唔好玩呀？

A: 喂！旅行好唔好玩啊？

B: The trip was fine but I'm not so fine now! The jet lag has messed up my sleep big time!

B: 嗰旅行就 OK，但係我而家就唔 OK 囉！啲時差攪和晒我瞓覺啲時間呀！

B: 這旅行就 OK，但是我現在就不 OK 啊！因為時差令我睡覺的時間一團糟啊！

<u>big time</u> – a lot

<u>Trip</u> – a short journey to a place and back quickly. 旅行 BUT

<u>Journey</u> – focuses more on travelling from one place to another, usually takes a longer time. 旅程

70. Skive off (phr v)– to avoid doing work - 蛇王，走堂 / 溜走，逃學

e.g.SC: After school, student A says to student B:

e.g.SC: 喺學校度，A 同 B 講：

e.g.SC: 在學校裏，A 跟 B 說：

A: Cathy is not here today – skiving off again?

A: Cathy 今日唔喺度喎，又走堂呀？

A: Cathy 今天不在啊，又逃學了？

B: Guess so!

B: 係啩！我想係囉！

B: 是啊！我想是吧！

e.g.SC: At the workshop, A and B talking about C:

e.g.SC: 喺工場度，A 同 B 講緊 C：

e.g.SC: 在工場裏，A 跟 B 說 C 的事情：

A: Where's John when we're so swamped with work?

A: 公司一多嘢做，阿 John 就唔知走咗去邊度㗎喇！

A: 公司有很多事情要做的時候，John 就不知道到哪裏去了！

B: Don't know – must have skived off!

B: 係喇！梗係去咗蛇王啦！

B: 對啊！一定是早早就溜走了！

swamped - explained in this book.

106

71. Suss something / somebody out (phr v) – to find out, understand about sth/sb - 睇穿，發覺，知，明白

e.g.SC: Two ladies A and B, talking about a man that A has been dating:

e.g.SC: 兩個女人講緊曾經同 A 拍過拖嘅男人：

e.g.SC: 兩個女人正在講 A 曾經約會過的男人：

A: So how's Chris? He seems to be a really nice guy!

A: 喂！Chris 點呀？佢睇起上嚟好似幾好咁喎！

A: 喂！Chris 怎麼樣啊？他看起來好像很好啊！

B: After going out with him a couple of times, I think I got him sussed. He's not the gentleman he's acting out to be!

B: 同佢出咗幾次街，我已經睇穿佢啦！佢唔係咁 gentleman 㗎咋！

B: 和他約會幾次，我已經看穿了他！他不是太君子的！

e.g.SC: At the workshop, a group of colleagues have been discussing how to go about a problem:

e.g.SC: 喺工場度，成班人諗緊點搞嗰問題：

e.g.SC: 在工場裏，一班人再考慮怎樣解決一個問題：

A: Any ideas people?

A: 有冇人有 idea 呀？

A: 有沒有人有辦法啊？

B: I think I've got it sussed! We should first....

B: 我諗我知點搞喇！我哋首先應該……

B: 我知道該怎麼樣做了！我們首先應該……

dating = going out with sb (explained in this book) 拍拖

guy = man – explained in this book

go about a problem = work on a problem 解決一個問題

I **got** it/him **sussed** (passive voice) (被動語態) = I've **sussed** it/him **out** (active voice) (主動語態)

72. That's life (idiom)– just the way things are: we have to accept them - 就係咁㗎喇 / 就是如此了

e.g.SC: At the office:

e.g.SC: 喺 office 度：

e.g.SC: 在 office：

A: Wow, that's just too much work!

A: 嘩！做死人咩，咁多嘢做㗎！

A: 嘩！忙死人不陪命呀，這麼多東西要做！

B: That's life!

B: 為搵食，就係咁㗎喇。

B: 為生活，就是如此了。

e.g.SC: 2 people waiting for the tube, and there's a delay:

e.g.SC: 兩個人等緊地鐵，架車遲嚟：

e.g.SC: 兩個人等地鐵，有延誤：

A: What! A delay! Just as we're in a rush!

A: 吓！要遲啲先到，仲趕時間添！

A: 吓！要遲一些才到，還趕時間啊！

B: That's life! There's never a train when you need one!

B: 就係咁㗎喇！趕時間要車嗰時就冇車！

B: 就是如此了！趕時間的時候，要車就沒有車！

或 **Such is life!**

73. Up somebody's street (idiom) – suitable for sb - 啱晒你啦 / 適合

e.g.SC: 2 friends shopping:

e.g.SC: 兩個朋友行緊街：

e.g.SC: 兩個朋友去購物：

A: Hey – you like Apple stuff, don't you? This magazine is up your street!

A: 喂！你咁鍾意 Apple 啲嘢，依本雜誌啱晒你啦！

A: 喂！你喜歡 Apple 的東西，這本雜誌很適合你啊！

B: I've already got it!

B: 我已經有喇！

B: 我已經有了！

e.g.SC: 2 friends chatting:

e.g.SC: 兩個朋友傾緊計：

e.g.SC: 兩個朋友聊天：

A: How's Philippe doing? Is he enjoying his new job?

A: 最近 Philippe 點呀？佢鍾唔鍾意份新工呀？

A: 近來 Philippe 怎麼樣啊？他喜歡那份新的工作嗎？

B: Oh, very much so! Environmental conservation is up his street.

B: 哦！超鍾意呀！環境保護啱晒佢啦！

B: 哦！很喜歡呀！環境保護很適合他的！

chatting explained in this book

Very much so! = very much! 超鍾意呀！很喜歡啊！

Up someone's avenue (US) (美式)

74. On the same page – (idiom) Same understanding on the topic being discussed - 你明白我，我明白你,有共通，大家都清楚明白

e.g.SC: In a company meeting, the team supervisor is talking to his/her team:

e.g.SC: 喺公司開緊會，嗰主任同緊佢班團隊講：

e.g.SC: 在公司開會中，主任和他們的團隊說：

A (supervisor): Just so we're on the same page, I'll give you a summary of our sales situation in the last quarter, and then I'll proceed to sales strategy. Is everyone ok with that?

A （主任）：為咗大家都清楚明白，我就將會比你哋總結上一個季度嘅銷售情況，之後我將會繼續制定一個銷售策略。大家 O 唔 OK 先？

A:（主任）：為了讓我們達成共識，我將向您總結上一季度的銷售情況，然後我將繼續制定銷售策略。大家都同意嗎？

B (all): Yup.

B（全部人）：好！

e.g.SC: 2 business partners talking about their project:

e.g.SC: 兩個做生意嘅 partner 講緊佢哋嘅 project：

e.g.SC: 兩個做生意的朋友正在討論他們的計劃:

A: Before we go further, can you tell me your ideas for this so far, so we're on the same page?

A: 喺我哋未講之前，可唔可以話俾我聽關於依個 project 你嘅 idea？睇吓我哋係唔係都有共通，以致大家都清楚明白。

A: 你可不可以說給我知道這個計劃裏你有什麼 idea？因為我們都要大家清楚明白的。

B: Yup, no problem. I was thinking…..

B: 好，冇問題，我就喺度諗…

B: 好，沒有問題。我正在想…

This idiom is similar in meaning to 'Up **to speed**', which means you have all the latest information, and are not falling behind. Both On the same page and Up to speed have the meaning of having information so one is prepared to do something.

這個成語的意思類似於 "up to speed"，這意味著您擁有所有最新資訊，並且不會落後。在同一頁面上和 "up to speed" 都具有擁有資訊的含義，因此準備做某事。

E.g. 2 parents talking about their child's school work e.g. 一對夫婦喺度講緊佢哋個仔嘅功課: 一對夫婦正在談論他們的兒子的功課:

A (mother): Johnny is falling behind…. A （媽咪）：Johnny 喺度退步緊…（媽媽）：Johnny 正在退步中…

B (father): Let's get him a tutor to get him up to speed with the other children in his class. B （爸爸）：不如搵個補習老師俾佢啦，等佢同其他同學程度都可以一樣咯！（爸爸）：幫他去找一個補習老師吧！讓他的程度和其他同學都可以一樣。

75. Cave in (phr v) - to give up – 屈服

e.g.SC: In a local cafe with a friend. A wants to lose weight by fasting, but today she's ordering a sweet cake. B is surprised and asks her:

e.g.SC: 喺茶餐廳度，A 想減肥，所以節食。但係今日佢叫咗蛋糕。B 就好出奇去問 A：

e.g.SC: 在茶餐廳裏，你正在減肥，所以 A 想節食。但是今天 A 點了一件蛋糕。B 很突然去問 A：

B: I thought you were fasting because you wanted to lose weight!

B: 你又話節食減肥，你仲食蛋糕！

B: 是你說節食減肥，但是你還是食蛋糕！

A: (sigh) Unfortunately, I caved in 2 days ago! Couldn't keep it up!

A: （唉）真係唔好彩我兩日之前已經忍唔住屈服咗㗎喇！真係 keep 唔到囉！

A：（唉）真是不好運，兩天前我已經忍不住屈服了！不可以繼續節食吧！

e.g.SC: Two friends watching a Netflix movie, and it's getting late:

e.g.SC: 兩個朋友睇緊 Netflix，而且都好夜喇：

e.g.SC: 兩個朋友正在看 Netflix，而且都很夜了：

A: Hey, let's find out the end of the story tomorrow- it's getting late, and I'm super tired!

A：喂！聽日先至睇埋個結尾啦！好夜㗎喇，我超劫呀！

A：喂！明天再看吧！現在很夜了！我很疲倦！

B: Sorry mate, I caved in last week and watched till the end! But I will watch it with you again - don't worry! Good night!

B: Sorry 呀，我上個禮拜已經忍唔住睇完結尾喇！但係我會同你再睇多次嘅！得㗎喇！早啲！

B: 不好意思啊，我上星期已經忍不住看完了！但是我會和你一起再看吧！晚安！

76. Have a word with someone - To talk it over with someone – 同佢講吓！- 和他/她說一下吧！

e.g.SC: A husband and wife talking about their daughter, and her homework:

e.g.SC: 兩公婆煩緊個女啲功課：

e.g.SC: 一對夫婦正在煩著他們的女兒的功課：

A (wife): Maybe you have a word with her - she won't listen to me.

A: （老婆）：你同佢講吓啦！佢都唔聽我講嘅！

A: （老婆）：你和她說一下吧！她不聽我的說的！

B (husband): Ok, I'll try.

B: （老公）：好，我試吓囉！

B: （老公）：好，我試試吧！

e.g.SC: At a university, after class:

e.g.SC: 喺大學度，啱啱上完堂：

e.g.SC: 在大學裏，下堂了：

A (lecturer): Simon, can I have a word with you?

A: （導師）：Simon，可唔可以同你傾吓？

A: （導師）：Simon，可不可以和你傾談一下？

B: (student): Sure, Mr Manor!

B: （學生）：哦，Mr Manor!

77. Ticking the box - to do what needs to be done because of rules and regulations – 求其寫，交功課（守則，規矩）

e.g.SC: On a street with lots of cars parked illegally. A traffic police is giving out parking tickets:

e.g.SC: 有好多違泊嘅車泊咗喺條街度，有個警察正在抄緊牌：

e.g.SC: 有很多違反泊車在這條街道上，有一個警察正在抄牌：

A: Wow, so many tickets were given out tonight! Where have you parked your car? Watch out. He's coming!

A: 嘩！今晚都有好多張抄咗喎！你架車泊咗邊度啊？睇住佢會過嚟呀！

A: 嘩！今晚有很多將已經抄了。你的車泊在哪裏？小心，他會過來啊！

B: Yeah, he's just box-ticking! But luckily I've parked my car in the car park tonight.

B: 係呀，佢要交數呀嘛！但係好彩今晚我泊咗架車喺停車場啫！

B: 對啊！他要交數嘛！但是今晚我行運了因為我泊了在停車場啊！

e.g.SC: Two friends talking about a visit to the GP (General Practitioner- family doctor):

e.g.SC: 兩個朋友傾緊去睇家庭醫生：

e.g.SC: 兩個朋友正在說去看家庭醫生:

A: What did the GP say about your stomach pain?

A: 你胃痛果度，醫生講咩？

A: 你胃痛怎麼樣？醫生說了什麼？

B: He asked me so many questions! Half of those questions were not related to my problem at all!

B: 佢問我好多嘢呀！有一半問題都唔關事嘅！

B: 他問我很多問題，有一半問題都不關這件事呢！

A: Oh, he was probably just ticking boxes!

A: 噢！佢可能淨係教功課啫！

A: 噢！他可能只是敷衍你吧！

78. You can bank on it - you're sure, confident it will happen/won't happen. You can rely on it - 肯定會/唔會發生

e.g.SC: At a company morning meeting, all the colleagues are waiting for the one staff member, who's usually late.

e.g.SC: 喺朝早公司開緊會，所有同事喺度等緊其中一個員工，佢成日遲到:

e.g.SC: 在早上公司正在開會中，所有的同事在等待其中一個員工，她常常遲到:

A: (manager): Good morning. Is everyone here?

A:（經理）：早呀！係咪所有人都到齊？

A:（經理）：早晨！是否所有人都在嗎？

B: (staff) Maggie is not here yet. She will arrive in the next 5 minutes.

B:（員工）：Maggie 仲未返喎。佢會 5 分鐘先到。

B:（員工）：Maggie 還未到啊！她會 5 分鐘才到。

C: (staff): Can't bank on it! She's usually super late!

C:（員工）：肯定佢唔會囉！佢成日都超遲㗎！

C:（員工）：肯定她不會的！她常常都會很遲啊！

e.g.SC: A husband and wife are talking:

e.g.SC: 一對夫婦喺度傾緊計：

e.g.SC: 一對夫妻正在傾談中：

A: (wife): Hubby, when you get a raise, we can buy the new car we wanted!

A:（老婆）：老公，如果你升職嘅話，咁我哋咪可以買部新車囉！

A:（老婆）：老公，如果你升職的話，這樣我們是否可以買一部新車呢？

B: (husband): Maybe at the end of this year honey! The boss promised me it'd be this year.

B:（老公）：可能要年尾喇！老細應承我話會今年嘅！

B:（老公）：可能要到年尾的時候啊！老闆答應我說會今年升職的！

A: (wife) I wouldn't bank on it- your boss always talks big!

A:（老婆）：我覺得肯定唔會囉！你老細淨係識講嘅啫！

A:（老婆）：我覺得肯定不會啊！你老闆只是說而已吧！

79. To have a brainwave –to have a sudden idea of what to do - 突然之間諗到個想法 / 突然知道該怎麼做

e.g.SC: 2 colleagues were talking about their project. They've been thinking of a problem for a while:

e.g.SC: 兩個同事喺度講緊嗰 project，佢哋諗緊有一個問題：

e.g.SC: 兩個同事正在談論一個 project，他們思考一個問題：

A: Ah I have a brainwave! We could…..

A: 吖！我有個 idea! 我哋可以…

A: 噢！我有一個 idea！我們可以…

B: That's a brilliant idea!

B: 嘩！正喎！

e.g.SC: Someone telling her friend about a problem she's been having:

e.g.SC: 有嗰人喺度向佢朋友講緊佢遇到的問題：

e.g.SC: 有人告訴她的朋友她一直遇到的問題：

A: I didn't know what to do, but I had a brainwave! I could ask YOU for help. So can you help me please?

A: 我唔知點做，但係我有嗰 idea! 我可以叫 '你' 幫吓手。咁你可唔可以幫吓我呀，唔該晒喎？

A: 我不知怎樣做，但是我有一個 idea！我可以問你幫幫手。這樣你可不可以幫我呢？拜託你啊！

B: Huh?! Me?!

B: 吓！我？！

80. Keep an eye /ear out for something (idiom) - to pay attention by looking (eye) or listening (ear) - 睇住/聽住, 看著/聽著

e.g.SC: At a car park:

e.g.SC: 喺停車場度：

e.g.SC: 在停車場裏：

A: Keep an eye out for a parking space ok?

A: 喂！你幫我睇吓有冇車位啦？

A: 喂！你幫我看一下有沒有車位？

B: Yep, on the job! (Meaning I'm doing it now)

B: 哦,睇緊!(意思係我而家做緊)

B: 啊!正在看!(意思是我現在正在做)

e.g.SC: At home, a mother is about to go out and is leaving some instructions for her daughter who's staying at home:

e.g.SC: 喺屋企度,媽咪想出街之前同嗰女講有啲野要佢做:

e.g.SC: 在家裏,媽媽想出去之前和她的女兒說有點事情要她做的:

A (mother): Daisy, I'm popping out for a moment. Could you keep an ear out for the doorbell? I'm expecting a delivery.

A(媽咪):Daisy,我出去一陣,你可唔可以幫我聽住嗰門鐘聲?有人會送貨嚟。

A(媽媽):Daisy,我出去一下,你可不可以幫我聽著門鐘聲?有人會來送貨。

B (daughter): OK, mum!

B(女):Ok 媽咪!

Chapter 3

Feelings words and Exclamations

感覺嘅字 普-感嘆嘅字

These are almost all adjectives or adjective phrases. 這些幾乎都是形容詞或形容詞短語

(Some of these are a little rude, so please use your discretion when using them. 其中一些有點粗俗, 使用時請小心)

81. Cheesed off / hacked off / peeved / bummed – annoyed, disappointed - 激氣，失望 / 生氣

e.g.SC: At a coffee shop, 2 teenagers talking:

e.g.SC: 喺茶餐廳度，兩個後生仔傾緊計：

e.g.SC: 在茶餐廳裏，兩個年青人正在聊天：

A: My mum woke me up so early yesterday! And it was Sunday!! I was so cheesed off!

A: 我媽咪尋日鬼死咁早叫我起身呀！仲要係禮拜日添！真係激死我呀！

A: 我媽媽昨天好早就叫我起床！還要是星期天！我真是很生氣啊！

B: I know! My mum does annoying things like that too!

B: 係囉！我媽咪成日都做埋啲咁嘅嘢㗎！

B: 對啊！我媽媽常常都會這樣做的！

e.g.SC: 2 football players talking after losing a match:

e.g.SC: 兩個足球員講緊佢哋啱啱輸咗嗰比賽：

e.g.SC: 兩個足球員談他們剛剛輸了的比賽：

A: So bummed we lost!

A: 輸咗好激氣呀！

A: 輸了，很生氣！

B: Yeah – we should have won! Bad luck!

B: 係啦！我哋應該贏㗎！真係唔好彩喇！

B: 對啊！我們應該贏的！真是不走運了！

To be **annoyed** + prep (**with**) sb – to be angry with sb 對人 BUT

To be **annoyed** + prep (**about**) sth – to be angry about sth 對事

He's really annoyed with his mother. 佢真係俾佢媽咪激激死。他真是對他的母親很生氣。

To **annoy**(v) – to make sb angry

To **bother**(v) – to disturb, to trouble 麻煩

He's really bothered his mother. 佢真係煩死佢媽咪。佢真是煩死他的母親。

To **bug** sb – to annoy sb 激人 令人生氣

to **piss sb off** (rude) 激一個人（粗俗）令人生氣（粗俗）

82. Chuffed to bits / thrilled to bits – extremely happy - 超開心 / 很開心

e.g.SC: In the school hall, B has just got her exam results:

e.g.SC: 喺學校大堂，B 啱啱收到張成績單：

e.g.SC: 在學校大堂，B 剛剛收到考試結果：

A: What are your results like?

A: 喂！啲成績點呀？

A: 喂！考試結果怎麼樣啊？

B: 9 As!! I'm chuffed to bits!

B: 九個 A 呀！我超開心呀！

B: 九個 A 呀！我很開心呀！

e.g.SC: 2 ladies talking. B's best friend from university is coming to visit from Australia:

e.g.SC: 兩個女仔講緊 B 喺澳洲大學最好嘅朋友嚟玩：

e.g.SC: 兩個女士講 B 的澳洲大學最好的朋友來旅遊：

A: Look at you! You're beaming!! Let me guess – Pauline's coming tomorrow, isn't she?

A: 睇吓你 4 萬咁嘅口，等我估吓先 — 聽日 Pauline 係唔係會到呀？

A: 看看你那麼開心，等我猜一猜 — 明天 Pauline 是不是會到啊？

B: Yeah! Thrilled to bits!!

B: 係呀！超開心呀！

B: 對啊！很開心啊！

To beam (v) – to have a big smile 4 萬咁嘅口, 開心

To beam + **at** somebody = to smile at sb. 向一個人笑

83. Crap (n) / crappy (adj) sth of poor quality, stupid or bad (mildly rude) - 垃圾，好屎，廢話，廢物（少少俗）很差

e.g.SC: A and B talking about C's arguments:

e.g.SC: A 同 B 講緊 C 嘅嘢：

e.g.SC: A 和 B 講 C 的事情：

A: What John said is a load of crap!

A: 阿 John 講嘅嘢全部都係一堆廢話！

A: John 講的事情，全部都是一堆廢話！

B: I know! Take it with a pinch of salt!

B: 係啦！唔好信晒佢呀！

B: 你說得對啊！別要完全相信他！

e.g.SC: A and B talking about the design of a product:

e.g.SC: A 同 B 講緊一個產品設計：

e.g.SC: A 和 B 正在談論一個產品的設計：

A: The design of the box is absolutely crappy. How do you expect it to sell?

A: 嗰盒嗰 design 咁屎？點賣呀？

A: 這個盒子的設計這麼差，怎麼樣賣呢？

A load of crap – rubbish talk 一堆廢話

Rubbish (英式) / **garbage** / **trash (US)美式**. 廢話，廢物

It's a rubbish movie, idea etc. 垃圾戲，想法 很差的電影，主意

Bollocks (UK)英式– vulgar(超俗) 廢話，廢物

Rubbish + at + v + ing + sth 做得唔好 / 好屎 做得不好/很差

I'm so **rubbish at** drawing. What don't you do it? 我畫畫咁屎，不如你畫啦！我畫畫很差，你畫吧！

煌庭
Bright Courtyard

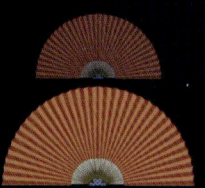

源自自然 品质纯正 天然美味

生活时尚集团始于2004年，总部位于中国上海，公司拥有千名员工、14家子公司，经营区域涉及伦敦、上海、宁波等地区。旗下拥有众多品牌至今公司已发展成以餐饮为主体，酒店民宿地产投资，公关运营与文化投资为两翼的服务休闲性综合企业。

伦敦分公司"煌庭会"自2011年创立，现已成为全英国规模最大中餐企业之一。坐落于贝克街，以现代粤菜和地道上海本帮菜为主，提供经典中式点心，花胶鸡火锅等特色菜肴，是您商务宴请和亲朋好友聚餐的理想场所。

地址：43-45 Baker Street, London, WLU 8EW
电话：02074866998

I know = You're right!!

84. Crummy – bad quality - 勁差 / 品質差

e.g.SC: A and B deciding where to have lunch:

e.g.SC: A 同 B 諗緊去邊度食 lunch：

e.g.SC: A 和 B 正考慮去哪裏食 lunch：

A: Where shall we go for lunch? Shall we go to Jo Jo's down in Soho?

A: 我哋去邊度食 lunch 好呀？不如去 Soho 嗰間 Jo Jo 吖？

A: 我們去哪裏吃午飯？去 Soho 那間 Jo Jo 吧！

B: No, not that crummy place!

B: 唔好啦！嗰間嘢勁差呀！

B: 不好啊！那間的食物品質很差呢！

A: But they do bubble tea there!

A: 但係嗰度有珍珠奶茶飲喎！

A: 但是那裏有珍珠奶茶喝啊！

e.g.SC: A and B talking:

e.g.SC: A 同 B 講緊：

e.g.SC: A 跟 B 說：

A: I went to Excel clinic for my checkup yesterday.

A: 我尋日去咗 Excel 診所度做身體檢查。

A: 我昨天去了 Excel 診所裏做身體檢查。

B: That crummy clinic! I have a better one. I'll give you the number for it next time.

B: 吓！嗰間嘢咁差！我有間仲好呀，下次俾個 number 你啦！

B: 吓！那間太差了！我知道有一間不錯的，下次給你電話號碼吧！

a **crummy** song = a badly written or sung song 勁差嘅歌 很差的歌

85. Daft – silly - 蠢，戇居 / 傻的

e.g.SC: 2 friends talking about somebody else:

e.g.SC: 兩個朋友講緊另一個人：

e.g.SC: 兩個朋友正在講另一個人：

A: How's your new colleague?

A: 你嗰新同事點呀？

A: 你的新同事怎麼樣啊？

B: Actually she's not as daft as she looks – she's an Oxford graduate!

B: 其實佢唔係睇起上嚟咁蠢㗎！佢喺 Oxford 畢業㗎！

B: 其實他不是看起來那麼蠢的！她是牛津大學畢業的啊！

e.g.SC: 2 friends talking about an argument B had with someone:

e.g.SC: 兩個朋友講緊關於 B 同人嘈交嘅事：

e.g.SC: 兩個朋友講關於 B 和人爭吵的事情：

A: So what did you say to Deanor then? After the little argument you had with him the other day?

A: 嘈完交之後，咁你點同 Deanor 講呀？

A: 吵完之後，你怎麼樣跟 Deanor 說啊？

B: I told him I didn't want to see him again.

B: 我同佢講，我唔想再見到佢囉。

B: 我跟他說，我不想再見到他了。

A: That's a pretty daft thing to say! He's in our group for the Science project – you'll have to see him anyway!

A: 唉！你點解咁戇居講啲咁嘅嘢呀！你明知佢喺我哋 Science project 嗰組裏邊。你實會見到佢㗎啦！

A: 唉！你為什麼說那麼傻的話！你知道他是在我們科學計劃的組裏邊。你一定會見到他的！

A colleague = a person who works with you. 同事

A college (UK)– a place where students go to study or receive training after they have left school. (英式) 學院

A college (US) -a university (美式) - 大學

129

pretty = quite 好, 的確

86. Dicey – dangerous - 危險

e.g.SC: A and B are hiring in the mountains. A says:

e.g.SC: A 同 B 行緊山，A 話：

e.g.SC: A 和 B 正在遠足，A 說：

A: Wow – look at this fog!

A: 嘩！好大霧呀！

A: 嘩！很大霧呀！

B: Oh dear! We should turn back – it's pretty dicey!

B: 哎呀係喎！都係唔好行喇！好危險呀！

B: 哎呀對啊！還是別走下去了！很危險啊！

e.g.SC: A and B talking about their investment:

e.g.SC: A 同 B 講緊佢哋啲投資：

e.g.SC: A 和 B 講他們的投資：

A: The stock is doing quite badly at the moment – pretty dicey to buy more. Think we should hold for now.

A: 而家啲市都幾差，買嗰隻貨都幾大風險。我諗我哋 hold 住先！

A: 現在的股市很差，買這一隻貨到風險很大。我覺得我們應該先持貨！

B: Yeah, you might be right, but one has to take some chances sometimes.

B: 係呀！你可能講得啱，不過有時我哋都要冒下險㗎！

B: 對啊！你可能說得對，不過我有時我們的冒險一下的！

87. Do somebody's head in – (phr v) – feel confused and annoyed - 搞到頭都暈埋，煩死

e.g.SC: At the office, A says to B:

e.g.SC: 喺公司度，A 同事同 B 同事講：

e.g.SC: 在公司裏，A 同事跟 B 同事說：

A: Golly, all this work!

A: 好鬼煩呀！咁多嘢要做！

A: 很煩！太多東西要做了！

B: I know – it's doing my head in!

B: 係啦！做到我頭都暈埋！

B: 對啊！做到我頭都暈了！

e.g.SC: 2 friends are trying to find a restaurant in Central at lunchtime:

e.g.SC: 兩個朋友喺中環搵緊餐廳食 lunch：

e.g.SC: 兩個朋友在中環正在找餐廳食 lunch：

A: Wow! So many people and cars! It's doing my head in!

A: 嘩！好鬼多人同好多車呀！搞到頭都暈埋！

A: 嘩！很多人和很多車子啊！令我頭很暈了！

B: Shall we just go to MacDonald's then?

B: 不如我哋去 M 記食算啦！

B: 我們去麥當勞食吧！

88. Gutted – extremely sad or disappointed - 非常失望

e.g.SC: 2 girlfriends shopping:

e.g.SC: 兩個女仔行緊街：

e.g.SC: 兩個女孩正在購物：

A: I'm gutted I didn't get the bag – shall we go back to that shop?

A: 我好失望，我冇買到嗰袋，不如去番間 shop 度啦！

A: 我很失望，我沒有買了那個袋子，我們回去那家店吧！

B: Huh? Do we really have to walk all the way back there again??

B: 吓！又要行番過去？？好遠喎!

B: 吓！又要回去？？很遠的!

e.g.SC: 2 friends chatting about something disappointing:

e.g.SC: 兩個朋友講緊好失望嘅嘢：

e.g.SC: 兩個朋友正在談論很失望的事情：

A: I'm gutted! If only I knew what I know now!

A: 唉！早知如果，何必當初呢！

A: 太糟糕了！早知如此，何必當初！

B: Shit happens! (vulgar)

B: 係啦！真係衰！（超俗）

B: 對啊！真是混蛋！（粗俗）

To have the guts / do a gutsy thing 夠薑 勇敢 **gut reaction/feel** 自然反應/感覺

e.g.SC: 2 friends doing a dare:

e.g.SC: A 大緊 B：

e.g.SC: A 對 B 說：

A: Bet you 10 bucks to have the guts to front up to him.

A: 如果你夠薑嘅話，三口六面同佢傾，就俾 10 皮你

A: 如果你勇敢的話，當面對他說，我就給你 10 塊

B: I'd do it for 20!

B: 你比 20 皮我就會做！

B: 你給 20 塊我就會做了！

e.g.SC: 2 friends talking about a friend who's returned something he's stolen:

e.g.SC: 兩個朋友講緊另一個朋友，還返偷咗嘅嘢：

e.g.SC: 兩個朋友談論另一個朋友，還回偷了的東西：

A: Wow! That was a gutsy thing to do!

A: 嘩！佢都幾夠姜喎！

A: 嘩！他都幾勇敢啊！

B: I know! Hats off to him!

B: 係啦！服咗佢喇！

B: 對啊！服了他了！

A: When he shouted at you, what did you do?

A: 佢鬧你嗰時，咁你點呀？

A: 他罵你的時候，你怎麼樣啊？

B: My gut reaction was to shout back, but I didn't do it as it'd only make things worse.

B: 我自然反應會鬧返佢轉頭囉。不過我冇咁做，因為會搞大件事。

B: 我自然反應，會罵回他吧。不過我沒有這樣做，因為會弄出大事。

Shit happens! (vulgar) = so bad! 真係衰！（超俗）

'**damn**' or '**bother**' are less rude words to mean the same thing. Damn 同 bother 係冇咁俗 damn 和 bother 是沒有那麼俗

bullshit (n) (vulgar)= nonsense talk 廢話（超俗） Can be shortened to 'BS'.

"Don't give me that **BS**!" 唔好同我講呢啲廢話喇！不要和我說那些廢話吧！

bucks = dollars 錢

Hats off – admire 佩服

89. Can / can't hack it (v)-can/can't handle it, take it - 忍受得到，唔到 / 忍受不到

e.g.SC: At home, A has been revising for his exams for a long time:

e.g.SC: 喺屋企，A 溫習咗好耐：

e.g.SC: 在家裏，A 溫習了很久：

A: Mum, I can't hack the revision anymore today. I'm going out for a walk to clear my head.

A: 媽咪，我今日唔可以再溫喇！我想出去行吓，relax 吓。

A: 媽媽，我今天不可以在溫習了！我想出去散步，輕鬆一下。

B: OK boy. Just don't take too long. Dinner will be ready in an hour's time.

B: 好啦仔！但係唔好行咁耐呀！一個鐘之後就食飯喇！

B: 行！但是不要去太久啊！一個小時之後就吃飯了！

e.g.SC: B has been advising A on his job problems:

e.g.SC: B 俾 A 一啲工作上嘅問題嘅意見：

e.g.SC: B 給 A 一些工作上的問題的意見：

A: I've been feeling so low lately! I hate my new job! It's just so boring!!

A: 我依排唔係好開心呀！我好憎我份新工囉！好悶呀！！

A: 我近來很不開心啊！我很討厭我的新工作呢！很悶啊！！

B: If you can't hack it, give it up! There's plenty more fish in the sea.

B: 如果你係忍受唔到嘅，就唔好做囉！出邊仲有大把工。

B: 如果你是忍受不到的，就不好做吧！外面還有很多工作可以做。

To clear one's head – to relax a bit 鬆弛吓 鬆弛一下

'If you can't stand the heat, get out of the kitchen' (idiom) 忍受唔到，就唔好做囉

90. Knackered – very tired, old or broken - 超劼，殘舊 / 很累

e.g.SC: After shopping all day, A says to B:

e.g.SC: A 買完嘢之後，A 同 B 講：

e.g.SC: A 買完東西之後，A 和 B 講：

A: I'm totally knackered! Been walking all day long to get this!

A: 嘩！我今日超劼呀！行咗成日買到依樣嘢！

A: 嘩！我今天很累啊！去了整天才買到這樣的東西！

B: So what have you got then?

B: 咁你買咗咩呀？

B: 你買了什麼？

e.g.SC: Just off work – at home, A tells his wife:

e.g.SC: 放咗工返到屋企，老公話：

e.g.SC: 放了工，回到家裏，老公說：

A: Honey, I'm so knackered! Had so much work today!

A: 唏！老婆，我今日超多嘢做呀，好鬼劼呀！

A: 老婆，我今天有很多事情要做，好累啊！

B: Oh dear! Go and grab a warm shower – it might just help.

B: 係呀！咁去沖個熱水涼先啦！

B: 是呀？！先去洗個熱水澡吧！

Too old or broken – e.g. This wallet's too **knackered**. I need to get a new one. e.g. 嗰銀包太舊喇，我要買個新㗎。這錢包太舊了，我要買一個新的。

To knacker (v) somebody – to make sb very tired. 令人好劫 令人很累

knackering (adj) – tiring 超劫 很累 **This job** is knacker**ing**. BUT **I'm** knacker**ed**. This difference is the same as in the word boring. e.g. "This movie is bor**ing**, BUT I'm bor**ed**." ing 同 ed 嘅分別：ing 對事，ed 對人

To grab a shower = to have a shower

91. A pain (n) – something inconvenient, difficult to do - 真係麻煩 / 真是麻煩

e.g.SC: 2 students talking about their coursework:

e.g.SC: 兩個學生講緊佢哋啲功課：

e.g.SC: 兩個學生正討論他們的功課：

A: Have you finished writing up the coursework?

A: 你做完未呀篇嘢？

A: 作業做好了沒有啊？

B: It was a pain! Took me ages to write it up!

B: 真係麻煩！我嘥咗好多時間去寫㗎！

B: 真是麻煩！我花了很多時間去寫啊！

e.g.SC: In a taxi, A has realized he's left his wallet at home:

e.g.SC: 喺的士度，A 發覺佢留低咗個銀包喺屋企：

e.g.SC: 在的士裏，A 發現他把錢包留在家裏：

A: Oh no! I've left my wallet at home! Sorry taxi driver – we need to go back! What a pain!

A: 唉！我留低咗個銀包，喺屋企度呀！唔好意思呀，司機！我哋要返返去喇！真係麻煩！

A: 唉！我樓下了錢包在家裏啊！不好意思啊，司機！我們要回去吧！真是麻煩了！

B: (taxi driver): Right-O!

B:（司機）：吓！OK 啦！

B:（司機）：行！

ages = a long time 好多時間

a pain in the arse (mildly rude) - 真係麻煩 (少少俗)

a painful person, an **annoying person** 一個好煩嘅人 一個很煩的人

Right-O = OK

92. Poorly (adj) / out of sorts / under the weather (adj phr) / run down (phr v) – not feeling well - 好差，唔舒服 / 很差，不舒服

e.g.SC: At work, A says to B:

e.g.SC: 開工嗰時，A 同 B 講：

e.g.SC: 工作時，A 和 B 說：

A: You don't look too good today! Are you alright?

A: 嘩！你面青青喎！你冇嘢吖嘛？！

A: 嘩！你面色很差啊！你還好吧？！

B: No, I feel poorly!

B: 係呀！唔係好舒服呀！

B: 對啊！不是太舒服啊！

e.g.SC: At school, teacher A says to student B:

e.g.SC: 喺學校，A 先生同啲同學講：

e.g.SC: 在學校，A 先生跟 B 同學說：

A: Sandy, you look out of sorts today – are you ok?

A: Sandy，你今日好似唔舒服喎！你冇嘢吖嘛？

A: Sandy，你今天好像不舒服啊！你沒有事吧？

B: I've been very tired lately.

B: 係啊！最近好劫呀！

B: 是啊！近來很累啊！

93. Chop chop! – quickly -嗱嗱聲 - 快一點吧

e.g.SC: 4 ppl have been waiting to play mahjong:

e.g.SC: 四個人等緊打麻雀:

e.g.SC: 四個人正在開始打麻雀:

A: Chop chop! Let's start! Remember whoever wins the game has to share the winnings!

A: 嗱嗱聲快啲開枱啦！記住邊一個贏咗錢，就要抽水㗎喇！

A: 快一點吧！記得誰贏了錢，是要拿錢出來食飯啊！

B, C, D: No problem!

B, C, D: 冇問題！

B, C, D: 沒有問題！

e.g.SC: 2 friends are walking to a bus stop. At a short distance the bus is coming:

e.g.SC: 兩個朋友行緊去巴士站，巴士就嚟到站:

e.g.SC: 兩個朋友正在行去巴士站，巴士差不多到的時候:

A: Don't look at your phone, chop chop! The bus is coming!

A: 你唔好再睇電話啦！嚤嚤聲啦！巴士嚟緊喇！

A: 你不好在看電話吧！快一點！巴士來了！

B: Woah yes, let's leg it!

B: 哦！咁我哋跑啦！

B: 對啊！我們跑吧！

<u>Leg it</u> explained in this book

94. Tacky - Cheap quality or in bad style - 好渣，寒酸/低俗，俗氣

e.g.SC: Inside a souvenir shop in London:

e.g.SC: 喺 London, 賣紀念品鋪頭：

e.g.SC: 在倫敦，一間賣紀念品的店舖內：

A: Have you found a gift for your mother-in-law yet?

A: 你搵唔搵到禮物送俾你外母未呀？

A: 你找不找到禮物送給你奶奶嗎？

B: Nah, they're all too tacky!

B: 冇呀，啲嘢都好渣！

B: 沒有啊！這間店全部東西都很低俗！

e.g.SC: 2 friends have just been to a Chinese restaurant in town:

e.g.SC: 喺唐人街，有兩個朋友去緊一間中餐廳：

e.g.SC: 在唐人街，有兩個朋友正在去一間中餐廳：

A: Did you see all the tacky decorations in there?

A: 喂！你見唔見到呢度啲裝修好鬼寒酸？

A: 喂！你見不見到這裏的裝修好低俗嗎？

B: Yes! The food was good though luckily!

B: 係呀！但係好彩啲嘢食都唔錯喎！

B: 對啊！但是很幸運地他們的食物都不錯啊！

95. It's dire! - it's bad, terrible, awful - 真係好屎/ 真是很差

e.g.SC: Some friends have been invited to a party but they are late. One of them explains:

e.g.SC: 有班朋友去緊個 party 不過佢哋遲到，其中一個人喺度講：

e.g.SC: 有一班朋友正在去一個 party，但是他們遲到，其中一個人正在說：

A: Sorry we're late, the traffic was dire! (Please don't say 'traffic jam' - literally no one uses it)

A: Sorry 我哋遲咗！出邊好塞車，情況好差呀！（冇人講 'traffic jam'）

A: Sorry 我們遲了！外面很塞車，情況很差呀！（沒有人會說 'traffic jam'）

B: Don't worry mate, come on, get a drink!

B: 算啦！嚟啦，飲杯嘢先啦！

B: 算吧！來吧！喝一杯酒啦！

e.g.SC: 2 friends chatting:

e.g.SC: 兩個朋友喺度傾緊計：

e.g.SC: 兩個朋友正在傾談中：

A: I would invite you to my house for dinner, but I'm a dire cook!

A: 我好想請你嚟食晚飯，不過我煮得好鬼屎㗎喎！

A: 我很想邀請你來吃晚飯，但是我的廚藝很差呢！

B: Don't worry, I'm pretty rubbish at it myself too! (pretty rubbish is the same as quite bad, not good - explained in this book)

B: 得啦！我都係煮得好屎㗎！（pretty rubbish 同好鬼屎一樣，唔好 - 喺 呢本書度解釋咗）

B: 不用擔心！我都是一樣煮得不好啊！（pretty rubbish 和相當差一樣，不好 -本書裏已經解釋了 ）

144

96. Absolutely! / Of course! / Sure! – good! - 好！當然啦！一定嘅！/ 行！

e.g.SC: A car salesperson B talking to a potential client A:

e.g.SC: B 車經紀，同緊 A 未來客人講：

e.g.SC: B 車經紀跟 A 未來客人說：

A: Thanks for that. I'll go away and think about it.

A: 唔該晒喎！我諗吓先啦！

A: 謝謝你啊！我先想一下！

B: Of course! Do give me a call if you want to test drive.

B: 好吖！當然啦！如果你想試車，隨時俾電話我吖！

B: 行！當然！如果你想是車子的話，任何時間都可以打電話給我的！

e.g.SC: 2 friends talking about some arrangements:

e.g.SC: 兩個朋友講緊嘅約會安排：

e.g.SC: 兩個朋友正在談一個約會安排：

A: So, that's it then. Let me know when you're free and we'll grab a nice lunch together.

A: 就係咁啦！你話俾我知你幾時得閒？，我哋去食 lunch 啦！

A: 就這樣了！你告訴我你什麼時間有空，我們去吃午飯！

B: Absolutely! I'll give you a buzz next week.

B: 一定！下個禮拜打俾你啦！

B: 一定！下個星期打電話給你！

Give someone a buzz = a telephone call, a ring 打電話俾人 打電話給別人

Grab lunch = get lunch 去食 lunch

97. Brilliant! / Smashing! / Excellent! / Lovely! / Awesome! / Beautiful! – very good - 好呀！超正呀！/ 極好！

e.g.SC: At a post office:

e.g.SC: 喺郵政局度：

e.g.SC: 在郵政局：

A: Can I have 2 local stamps please?

A: 唔該我想要兩個本地郵票？

A: 麻煩你，我想要兩枚本地郵票？

B: Here. That'll be two pounds please.

B: 嗱！兩磅吖，唔該！

B: 給你！兩磅吧，謝謝！

A: (Takes the stamps) Smashing! Thanks very much.

A:（拎住啲郵票）好呀！唔該晒！

A:（拿了郵票）好啊！謝謝！

e.g.SC: A has watched a movie. B wants to know how it was:

e.g.SC: A 睇咗套戲，B 想知好唔好睇：

e.g.SC: A 看了一套電影，B 想知道好不好看：

A: How was the movie?

A: 套戲點呀？

A: 這齣電影什麼樣啊？

B: It was brilliant! You should see it.

B: 超正喎！你要去睇喇！

B: 極好啊！你得看看了！

e.g.SC: At the supermarket checkout:

e.g.SC: 喺超級市場，收銀處度：

e.g.SC: 在超市，收銀處裏：

A: (cashier): That'll be 25 pounds please.

A:（收銀員）：25 英鎊，唔該。

A:（收銀員）：25 英鎊，謝謝。

B: (customer): OK, here you go. (handing the money to the cashier)

B:（客）：好呀，嚤！（俾緊錢嗰收銀員）

B:（客）：這是你要的！（付錢給收銀員）

A: Would you like a bag?

A: 要唔要袋呀？要不要袋子？

B: Yes, please – that'd be good.

B: 好喔，唔該！好啊，謝謝！

A: Here you are.

A: 嚤！給你。

B: Lovely – thanks.

B: 好嘅，唔該！好了，謝謝！

A: Would you like me to bag it for you?

A: 要唔要幫你袋埋佢？

A: 要不要幫你袋起來嗎？

B: No thanks, I'm fine.

B: 唔使喇！我得㗎喇！

B: 不用！我這就行了！

In Chinese, we have very few of these positive responses apart from 'good'. 中文正面嘅答案比較少,除咗 '好呀!'

In English, it's very normal and polite to use positive response expressions with very simple actions like receiving a parcel from the postman, or getting change from a supermarket cashier. 英國人喜歡用好有禮貌客氣嘅正面回覆.

I'm fine = I'm OK. I can do it. I don't need help 我得㗎喇 我可以了

"**I'm fine thanks**" is a polite way of saying, "I don't want sth anymore." 我唔想再要喇 （禮貌啲嘅講法）我不想再要了（禮貌的說法）

98. Sick! / appalling! / dreadful! / awful! / annoying! / a nightmare! – very bad - 好差！恐怖！很差！

e.g.SC: A father-in-law is talking on the phone with his daughter-in-law who lives in Singapore:

e.g.SC: 岳父同新加坡個家嫂傾緊電話：

e.g.SC: 岳父正和新加坡的家嫂在談電話：

A: (father-in-law): So, how's the weather over there?

A:（岳父）：你嗰邊嘅天氣點呀？

A:（岳父）：你那邊的天氣怎麼樣？

B: It's dreadful – raining all the time!

B: 好差呀！成日都落雨！

B: 很差啊！常常都下雨！

e.g.SC: In a singing competition, someone is singing:

e.g.SC: 喺唱歌比賽度，有嗰人唱緊歌：

e.g.SC: 在唱歌比賽中，有一個人在唱歌中：

A: (whispers): Awful! Don't think I can sit through this. Excuse me, off to the loo.

A:（細細聲）：唉呀，唱得好恐怖呀！我唔聽喇！唔該借借！我去一去廁所先！

A:（少少聲）：唉呀，太難聽了！我不聽了！不好意思啊！我先去洗手間！

B: Don't be rude! You can't walk out now!

B: 唔好咁冇禮貌啦！你而家唔可以行出去㗎！

B: 不要這麼沒有禮貌吧！你現在不可以出去的！

'**Raining all the time**!' **Raining** here is the – ing form of '**it was raining.**' In spoken English, it's sometimes ok to take away 'it is or it was', especially at the beginning of a sentence.

這裡的 "Raining" 是在 "it was raining" 的 -ing 形式。在英語口語中，有時可以去掉 "it is" or "it was"，尤其是在句首。

99. Crud! / Gross! – to refer to disgusting or unrefined acts or things - 超核突！好肉酸！/ 很討厭的！很難看！

e.g.SC: In B's university dorm, A comments on some posters of monsters on the wall:

e.g.SC: 喺 B 嗰大學宿舍度，牆身貼咗幾張怪獸嘅 poster，A 講：

e.g.SC: 在 B 的大學宿舍裏，牆身貼了幾張怪獸的海報，A 說：

A: Did you put these posters up? They're gross!

A: 你放上去㗎啲 poster？好肉酸喎！

A: 是你放上去的海報嗎？很討厭啊！

B: Don't you like them? I think they're funny!

B: 你唔鍾意咩？我覺得佢哋幾得意呀！

B: 你不喜歡嗎？我覺得他們很可愛啊！

e.g.SC: On the street. I saw a man wearing a suit picking his nose:

e.g.SC: 喺條街度，A 見到條西裝友撩緊鼻屎：

e.g.SC: 在街上，A 見到一個穿着西裝的男人挖鼻孔：

A: Oh my! Look at that smart–looking man. He's picking his nose!

A: 唉喲！睇吓條西裝友，佢撩緊鼻屎呀！

A: 唉喲！看一下這個西裝男人，他挖鼻孔啊！

B: Crud!

B: 嘩！超核突呀！

B: 嘩！很難看的！

Picking one's nose 撩鼻屎 挖鼻孔 – to put one's finger into the nostril.

"**That's crud/gross**!" – The stress must be on the word 'crud/gross' 喺'crud' 同'gross' 度加重語氣表達驚訝。在 'crud' 和'gross' 裏加重語氣表達驚訝。

100. Flipping heck! (mildly rude) / Bloody hell! (rude) – to express annoyance or anger - 頂佢吖！（少少俗），（粗俗）/ 該死的！（粗俗）

e.g.SC: 2 friends talking about someone else:

e.g.SC: 兩個朋友講緊另一個人：

e.g.SC: 兩個朋友正在談別人：

A: Flipping heck! Matthew didn't even say a word of thanks, after all the trouble he's put me to!

A: 頂佢吖！我同 Matthew 做咗咁多嘢，一句多謝都冇！

A: 該死的！我和 Matthew 做了那麼多的事情，一句謝謝都沒有！

B: Ungrateful wanker! (rude)

B: 忘恩負義，衰人嚟㗎！（粗俗）

B: 忘恩負義，正王八蛋！（粗俗）

e.g.SC: At the restaurant:

e.g.SC: 喺餐廳度：

e.g.SC: 在餐廳裏：

A: Bloody hell! (rude) What kind of service is this?

A: 頂佢吖！（粗俗）咩服務態度呀？

A: 該死的！什麼服務態度呀？

B: Let's take it up with the manager!

B: 叫經理嚟同我哋講！

B: 叫經理來跟我們講！

To put somebody to a lot of trouble = to cause sb trouble = to **bother** sb 比一個人好多麻煩 給一個人很多麻煩

to save somebody the trouble of doing something 幫你做一啲嘢等到你唔使煩 幫你做一點東西，以致你不必煩

e.g. I can get the milk for you on my way if you like, to save you the trouble of going out. e.g. 我可以返嚟嗰時買埋奶，咁你咪唔使出街囉 我可以回來的時候買牛奶，那你不用外出吧！

101. For crying out loud! – to express annoyance - 激死喇！/ 氣死了！

e.g.SC: A is fiddling with the printer that has suddenly stopped working:

e.g.SC: 你嘅 printer 突然間唔 work。A 喺度搞緊佢：

e.g.SC: A 的 printer 突然間不動。A 正在弄它：

A: For crying out loud! What is wrong with this stupid printer? Just as I need it to work!

A: 激死人喇！點解咁衰無啦啦唔 WORK 㗎！我就係要 PRINT 嘢呀！

A: 氣死人啦！搞什麼鬼動啊！我就是要打印呀！

B: Look, the plug has gone loose! Pussy must have knocked it out of the socket.

B: 睇吓個插頭鬆咗呀！梗係隻貓整鬆咗啦！

B: 看一下這插座鬆了啊！一定是那隻貓兒弄鬆了！

e.g.SC: A couple is in a hurry to leave the house to get somewhere. The dog has just knocked some coffee onto the floor, leaving a stain on the carpet:

e.g.SC: 一對夫婦，趕住出門口，隻狗又整寫咗杯咖啡落張地氈度：

e.g.SC: 一對夫婦趕出去，那隻狗有碰倒杯咖啡在地氈上：

A: (wife): Oh no!!

A:（老婆）：o……唉呀！！

B: (husband): For crying out loud!! Monty! Stop wagging that tail! Can't afford another spillage!

B:（老公）：激死人喇！Monty！唔好再擺尾喇！你唔可以再整瀉㗎喇！

B:（老公）：氣死人啦！Monty！不要再搖尾巴！你不可以再碰到東西了！

102. Give me a break! – stop doing / saying sth because it is annoying or unbelievable (satirical) - 唔該你啦！（諷刺）/ 別要這樣吧！（諷刺）

e.g.SC: At home, a mother is telling his teenage son to have a haircut:

e.g.SC: 喺屋企度，媽咪叫嗰仔去剪頭髮：

e.g.SC: 在家裏，媽叫兒子去理髮：

A: (mother): Edward, you really need a haircut. Your hair is down to your collar!

A:（媽咪）：Edward，你真係要剪頭髮喇！你啲頭髮長到落條衫領度喇！

A:（媽媽）：Edward，你真是要去理髮啊！你的頭髮長到衣領上啊！

B: (son): Give me a break, mum! I'll get round to it!

B:（仔）：唉！媽咪！唔該你啦！我有時間就會去做㗎啦！

B:（兒子）：唉！媽咪！別要這樣吧！我有時間的話就會去做了！

e.g.SC: 2 friends talking:

e.g.SC: 兩個朋友傾緊計：

e.g.SC: 兩個朋友正在聊天：

A: My old teacher's mother is 130 years old!

A: 我舊老師個媽咪成130歲喇！

A: 我以前的老師的媽咪都有130歲了！

B: 130 years old! Give me a break! That's impossible!

B: 130歲！！唔該你啦！根本冇可能！

B: 130歲！！別要這樣吧！根本不可能的！

Cut me some slack (US) (美式)

I'll get round to it – I'll do it when I have time, eventually 我有時間就會做㗎喇！我有時間的話就會做了吧！

103. Have had it! – going to experience sth bad, unable to accept a situation anymore - 玩完喇！夠喇！/ 玩完了！夠了！

e.g.SC: 2 teenage brothers are talking:

e.g.SC: 兩個兄弟講緊嘢：

e.g.SC: 兩個兄弟在說：

A: You've scratched Dad's car! You've had it!

A: 你死喇！你撞花咗你老竇架車！你今次玩完喇！

A: 你死定了！你撞花了爸爸的車！你今次玩完了！

B: Don't tell!

B: 唔好報串呀！！

B: 不要告密啊！！

e.g.SC: In the office:

e.g.SC: 喺 office 度：

e.g.SC: 在 office 裏：

A: I've had it! I'm up to here with work. I need a break!

A: 唉！夠喇！我做夠喇！我需要唞吓！

A: 唉！夠了！我做夠了！我需要休息一下！

B: Go and get yourself a cup of tea!

B: 咁去飲杯茶先啦！

B: 你先去喝杯茶吧！

'<u>Have had it</u>' is an expression, but the word 'have' is the verb in the expression, so it needs to agree with the subject. Have had it」是一個表達，但「have」這個字是表達中的動詞，所以它需要與主詞一致。

e.g. <u>I've</u> had it. <u>She's</u> had it. 我已經受夠了。 她已經受夠了。

104. Not give a monkey's! – not care about sth/sb, or not interested at all - 話之佢！/ 不用理會！完全不在乎！

e.g.SC: A husband and wife talking about the husband's elderly mother:

e.g.SC: 一對夫婦講緊關於丈夫嘅年老媽媽：

e.g.SC: 一對夫婦靜講關於丈夫的年老媽媽：

A: (wife): Honey, you can't just sell your mother's old furniture without asking her first!

A: （老婆）：老公，你唔可以冇問過阿媽就買咗佢啲舊傢俬㗎！

A: （老婆）：老公，你不可以沒有問過媽媽就買了她的舊傢俬啊！

B: (husband): Honestly, I don't give a monkey's! She's always hoarding things!

B:（老公）：講真，我話之佢啦！佢成日 keep 住啲嘢都唔掟！

B:（老公）：我是不會理會她的！她常常保留東西都不掉！

e.g.SC: 2 friends talking about B's ex-girlfriend:

e.g.SC: 兩個朋友講緊關於 B 嘅前度女友：

e.g.SC: 兩個朋友講關於 B 的前度女朋友：

A: Hey, I saw Jackie in the club last night! She was asking about you.

A: 喂！尋晚喺 group 度，我見到 Jackie 喎！佢有問你啲嘢呀。

A: 喂！昨晚在會所裏，我見到 Jackie 啊！她有問起你的事情啊。

B: Frankly, I don't give a monkey's! Did you tell her to get lost?

B: 老實講吖！我話之佢啦！咁你有冇叫佢行開啲呀？

B: 講真一點！我是完全不在乎的！那你有沒有叫他走開？

e.g.SC: Outside the pub:

e.g.SC: 酒吧出邊：

e.g.SC: 酒吧外邊：

A: Got any fags?

A: 有冇煙呀？

A: 有沒有香煙啊？

B: Bugger off! (rude) Get a job!

B: 死開啦！(粗俗) 搵份工啦！

B: 死開！(粗俗) 去找一份工作吧！

I don't give a monkey's + **about** sth 話之佢, 完全不在乎

I don't give a damn + **about** sth (rude) 話之佢, 完全不在乎 (粗俗)

I don't give a shit + **about** sth (vulgar) and **I don't give a toss** + **about** sth (vulgar) 話之佢 (超俗), 完全不在乎 (很粗俗)

e.g. **I don't give a damn about (slightly rude 少少俗)** how he feels, after what he's done to me. 我話知佢嘅感受吖，佢對我咁差。 我是不會理會他的感受，他對我太差了。

hoard = collect and keep, keep 住, 積

To get lost = to go away (mildly rude) 走開 (少少俗)

Piss off! (rude) 死開 (俗, 粗俗)

Bugger off! (vulgar) and **fuck off** (vulgar) 死開 (超俗, 很粗俗)

Frankly = honestly, seriously 老實講, 講真

To bugger something up – to break or spoil sth 搞禍, 弄壞 (俗)

e.g. Don't **bugger up** the project or we're in big trouble!

e.g. 唔好搞禍咗 project 呀，唔係就大鑊喇！ 不好，弄壞這個 project 啊，如果不是就大件事了！

To be pissed – to be drunk (mildly rude) 飲醉酒, 喝醉（少少俗）

e.g. Did you see Lesley last night? She was so pissed!

e.g. 尋晚你有冇見到 Lesley 呀？佢飲得好醉呀！昨晚你有沒有看到 Lesley 嗎？她喝得很醉啊！

105. Oh my gosh (god)! / golly! – to express surprise, excitement or fear - 哎喲！/ 我的天呀！

e.g.SC: 2 friends are taking a walk in the countryside:

e.g.SC: 兩個朋友郊外地方散緊步：

e.g.SC: 兩個朋友在郊外地方散步：

A: Oh my gosh! There's a dead monkey over there! (surprise)

A: 哎喲！嗰度有隻死馬騮呀！（O 嘴）

A: 我的天呀！那邊有一隻死了的馬騮啊！（驚訝）

B: Oh no! So sad! I wonder what's happened to it!

B: O……NO！好慘呀！發生咩事呢？

B: 很不幸呀！發生什麼事呢？

e.g.SC: A has just come out from the toilet. She doesn't know that B is right behind her:

e.g.SC: A 啱啱去完廁所。佢唔知道 B 喺佢後邊：

e.g.SC: A 剛剛去洗手間。他不知道 B 在他的後邊：

A: Oh my gosh! Why did you suddenly jump out of nowhere? You scared me to death!

A: 哎喲！你喺邊度突然間走出嚟㗎？你嚇死我喇！

A: 哎喲！你在哪裏突然間走出來？你嚇死我了！

B: Ha! Ha!

B: 哈！哈！

Please don't use 'oh my god' if you or the listener is religious.

如果您或聽眾有宗教信仰，請不要使用 'oh my god'.

Sth/sb that/who is **dead** 死咗 死了 (focus is on the result) 結果 BUT

Sth/sb **died** yesterday 死咗 死了 (focus is on the time) 時間

Also, '**Crikey**!' = 'Oh dear!' 哎喲！我的天呀！

e.g. "**Crikey**! What time is it? Need to run!" 哎喲！咁晏喇！要閃喇！我的天呀！那麼晚了？！要走了！

106. What on earth?! / What the heck?! / What the hell?! – words for emphasis (mildly rude) - 究竟？話之佢啦！（少少俗）/ 搞什麼鬼？不用理會了！（少少俗）

e.g.SC: B has just broken up with his girlfriend and is looking at a photograph of them together:

e.g.SC: B 同佢女朋友，啱啱分咗手，正睇緊佢哋嘅合照：

e.g.SC: B 和他女朋友，剛剛分了手，正在看他們的合照：

A: (about to tear up the photo): Harry, what the hell do you think you're doing?!

A:（想撕咗張相）Harry，你究竟喺度搞咩呀？

A:（想撕掉了一張相片）Harry，你搞什麼鬼啊？！

B: Mandy and I are finished – no point keeping this!

B: Mandy 我已經玩完喇！依啲嘢我都唔使再 keep 住啦！

B: Mandy 和我已經完了！這些東西我都不需要了！

e.g.SC: A is inviting his friend to go to watch a late movie with him:

e.g.SC: A 邀請緊佢朋友一齊去睇午夜場：

e.g.SC: A 邀請他朋友一起去看午夜場：

A: Steven, want to watch Mission Impossible this Friday night? There's a discounted late night showing at Odeon.

A: Steven，星期五晚想唔想去睇 Mission Impossible 呀？喂 Odeon 午夜場有 discount 喎！

A: Steven ，星期五晚想不想去 Mission Impossible 啊？UA 午夜場有折扣啊！

B: (thinking) Mmm – my parents don't really want me to go out late at night, but what the heck! There's nothing happening on Saturday – yeah ok – let's go!

B:（諗緊）嗯……我屋企人唔想我出夜街㗎，不過話之佢啦！橫掂我星期六都冇街去，OK啦！我哋去啦！

B:（正在想）嗯……我家人不想我晚出啊，但是不用理會了！我星期六都不外出，OK！我們去吧！

107. Have a go at someone - to criticize someone - 批評，指責

e.g.SC: A mother is talking to her teenage son about the state of his bedroom:

e.g.SC: 媽媽喺度同嗰仔講緊佢間房：

e.g.SC: 媽媽正在和他的兒子談論他的房間：

A (mother): Danny, look at your room! Tidy it up!

A:（媽媽）：Danny，睇吓你間房！執好佢啦！

A:（媽媽）：看看你房間！執拾一下吧！

B: Ok ok mum! Stop having a go at me all the time!

B: 得啦！呀媽！唔好成日挑剔我啦！

B: 好的！媽媽！不好時常指責我吧！

e.g.SC: 2 restaurant chefs talking about their manager in the kitchen:

e.g.SC: 喺廚房度，兩個餐廳廚師喺度講緊關於佢哋個經理：

e.g.SC: 在廚房裏，兩個餐廳廚師正在談論關於他們的經理：

A: Boss is always having a go at me about the dishes being too salty!

A: 老細成日喺度話我整啲餸好鹹咯！

A: 老闆時常在這裏說我做的餸很鹹的！

B: Is that so?! Then you'd better put less salt!

B: 真係咁呀？！咁你最好落少啲鹽喇！

B: 真的嗎？！這樣你最好給小一點鹽吧！

Chapter 4

To Tell Somebody Off

鬧嘅字, 表示不滿的詞

(Some of these are rude so please use your discretion when using them. 其中一些粗俗, 使用時請小心)

108. Ask for it – to deserve something bad because sb didn't listen to advice – 攞嚟衰 / 自找麻煩

e.g.SC: 2 friends are talking about their friend C, who has failed his exams:

e.g.SC: 兩個朋友講緊 C 朋友考試肥佬：

e.g.SC: 兩個朋友正談 C 朋友考試不合格：

A: Frank was asking for it, partying the night before the exams!

A: 呀 Frank 佢自己攞嚟衰，考試前一晚仲去 party。

A: Frank 他自己找麻煩的，考試前一晚還去派對。

B: How silly!

B: 佢真係蠢！

B: 他真笨！

e.g.SC: 2 good girlfriends speaking on the phone:

e.g.SC: 兩個女仔好朋友，正在傾緊電話：

e.g.SC: 兩個女朋友正在談電話：

A: How are you – still sick?

A: 你點呀？仲好唔舒服呀？

A: 你怎麼樣啊？還很不舒服嗎？

B: Yeah unfortunately. I still went for my yoga yesterday though.

B: 係呀！但係我尋日仲去上 yoga 添。

B: 對啊！但是我昨天還去上瑜伽班啊。

A: You've asked for it honestly. You should be resting!

A: 講真，你自己攞嚟衰㗎！你應該去休息吓嘛！

A: 你真的自找麻煩啊！你應該好好休息一下吧！

109. Bonkers / mental / (stark) raving mad / barmy (adj) / a basket case / a moron / a nutter (n) – crazy, out of sb's mind - 黐線，傻 / 瘋子，傻子(些粗俗)

e.g.SC: A has been waiting to see a doctor for an hour:

e.g.SC: A 等緊睇醫生，已經等咗一粒鐘：

e.g.SC: A 等看醫生，已經等了一個小時：

A: I think I'll go bonkers if I have to wait any longer. Nurse, I …

A: 等咗成粒鐘，仲等我就嚟黐線㗎喇！姑娘，我……

A: 等了一個小時，還未到我，我就快瘋了！護士，我……

e.g.SC: A is driving really fast, B is scared:

e.g.SC: A 飛緊車，B 好驚就話：

e.g.SC: A 開車開得很快，B 嚇壞了，說：

B: You're absolutely mental driving that fast!

B: 喂！你開得咁快，你黐㗎！！

B: 喂！你開車開得那麼快，你瘋了嗎！！

A: Wah wee!

A: 哈哈……

B: Stop it! You moron!!

B: 唔好開得咁快啦！你黐線㗎！！

B: 別開得那麼快啦！你瘋了！！

'**go mental**' – be very angry 發爛渣 很生氣

e.g. My mum will **go mental** if she finds out I've failed my exams.
e.g. 如果我媽咪知道我考試肥佬，佢實會發哂爛渣㗎！如果我媽媽知道我考試不合格，她一定會很生氣的！

110. A fibber (n) / tell fibs (v) – a liar, to tell lies about sth not too important - 講大話，大話精 / 撒謊的人

e.g.SC: A talking to B:

e.g.SC: A 同 B 講：

e.g.SC: A 跟 B 說：

A: Karen, don't believe a word of what Ben says whatever you do – he's a real fibber!

A: Karen！你點都唔好信阿 Ben 講啲嘢呀！佢正大話精嚟㗎！

A: Karen！你怎樣都不好相信阿 Ben 說的話啊！他是愛撒謊的！

e.g.SC: 2 friends talking:

e.g.SC: 兩個朋友講緊嘢：

e.g.SC: 兩個朋友在談話中：

A: Come on! Don't fib! Where were you last night? Been calling you all night!

A: 喂！唔好講大話啦！你尋晚究竟去咗邊？成晚打俾你呀！

A: 喂！不好撒謊了！你昨晚究竟去了哪裏？整天打電話給你啊！

B: With my friend Jasmine! Who else?!

B: 咪同我 friend Jasmine 有邊個啫？！

B: 跟我的朋友 Jasmine 一起啊！還有誰呢？！

"**Come on!**" can be used in front of any of these exclamations. 喂！

e.g. "**Come on! Give me a break!**" Or 喂！唔該你啦！喂！別這樣吧！

e.g. "**Come on! Don't fib!**" 或 喂！唔好講大話啦！不好撒謊了！

111. Give somebody an earful / give somebody a piece of one's mind – to tell sb you're very unhappy about sth/sb - 鬧人（鬧死，爆）/ 罵人（罵死）(些粗俗)

e.g.SC: A and B talking about the argument A had with C:

e.g.SC: A 同 B 講緊關於 A 同 C 嘈交啲嘢：

e.g.SC: A 和 B 談關於 A 和 C 爭吵的事情：

A: If Brandon dares to come and face me, I'll give him an earful!

A: 如果 Brandon 再夠膽嚟見我呢！我就會鬧爆佢㗎喇！

A: 如果 Brandon 再咁來面對我呢！我就會罵死他了！

B: I think he's probably avoiding you!

B: 我諗佢可能避開緊你啦！

B: 我想他可能正在避開你了！

e.g.SC: At a department store, A is making a complaint:

e.g.SC: 喺百貨公司度，A 投訴緊：

e.g.SC: 在百貨公司裏，A 正在投訴：

A: What kind of service is this? I want to see the manager and give him a piece of my mind!

A: 嘩！依度咩服務呀？我想見經理，鬧爆佢都好呀！

A: 嘩！這裏什麼服務呀？我想見經理，罵他一頓！

112. Give somebody the two fingers / give somebody a bollocking – to express anger at sb (vulgar) - 問候佢，媽叉佢（超俗）/ 他媽的，咒罵（很粗俗）

e.g.SC: 2 friends talking:

e.g.SC 兩個朋友講緊：

e.g.SC: 兩個朋友正在說：

A: Frankie – I'm gonna get a bollocking from Eddie! – I've crashed his car!

A: Frankie，我今日好黑仔呀！我撞咗 Eddie 部車呀！佢一定會媽叉我囉！

A: Frankie，今天我很倒楣啊！我撞了 Eddie 的車！他一定會他媽我的！

B: Oh oh! You're doomed!

B: 啊！啊！你大鑊喇！

B: 啊！啊！你死定了！

e.g.SC: On the beach. A group of boys are making passes at 2 girls:

e.g.SC: 喺沙灘度，有班男仔溝緊兩個女仔：

e.g.SC: 在沙灘裏，有一班男人正在勾搭兩個女子：

A: Look at those losers – wish they'd just leave us alone!

A: 睇吓班麻甩佬，希望佢哋快啲走開啦！

A: 看這班廢物，希望他們快快走開吧！

B: I know. I'm going to give them the two fingers in a minute!

B: 係啦！我就嚟去媽叉佢哋㗎啦！

B: 對啊！我快要咒罵他們了！

gonna get = going to get

doomed = in trouble 大鑊,死定

make passes = get attention from the opposite sex - 引起異性關注

losers - explained in this book

113. Give someone a mouthful - to shout angrily at someone. (a little offensive) -媽叉，鬧人，罵人 (些粗俗)

e.g.SC: A person is driving his friend through a park, and there are too many cyclists in the park, so the driver complains to his friend:

e.g.SC: A 揸緊車，同佢朋友經過公園，而且有好多踩單車啲人，揸車嗰個就喺度同個 friend 埋怨：

e.g.SC: A 和她的朋友一起正在揸車，經過公園，而且有很多踏單車的人，司機和她的朋友投訴：

A: These cyclists take up almost the whole road!

A: 啲單車呀！爆哂成條路囉！

A: 這些單車真的很多，完全用了這條路！

B: If they come too close to your car, give them a mouthful!

B: 如果佢哋一揩親你部車，你就媽叉佢哋囉！

B: 如果他們碰到你的車，你就罵他們吧！

e.g.SC: In the changing room of a sports hall.

e.g.SC: 喺運動場度喺更衣室：

e.g.SC: 在運動場裏在更衣室內：

A: We'd better hurry up, or the coach will give us a mouthful!

A: 喂，我哋快啲啦，果唔係教練會鬧我哋㗎啦！

A: 喂，我們要快一點吧！遲了，教練會罵我們的！

B: Yeah, we'd better!

B: 係呀，會快㗎啦！

B: 是啊！會快一點吧！

173

114. Suck up to someone - to make someone like you by saying or doing something they like - 攞著數/取人便宜

e.g.SC: After a lesson at university, 2 students are talking about their friend who is offering to help his lecturer gather up his papers:

e.g.SC: 喺大學度，啱啱上完堂，兩個學生喺度講緊佢哋嗰朋友，話佢成日幫嗰導師收功課：

e.g.SC: 在大學裏，剛剛上完堂，兩個學生正在談論他們的朋友，說他時常幫教師收集功課：

A: Look at him, he's sucking up to the lecturer!

A: 睇吓佢啦！佢想搵導師著數囉！

A: 看看他！他想找導師便宜啊！

B: Yeah, that's just too obvious!

B: 係呀！睇得出啦！

B: 對啊！看得出來啦！

e.g.SC: In a shop, 2 staff members are talking about another employee:

e.g.SC: 喺鋪頭度，兩個員工喺度講緊其他同事嘅嘢：

e.g.SC: 在店裏，兩個員工正在談論其他同事的事情：

A: Wow, look at the way she sucks up on the boss!

A: 嘩！睇吓佢一定係想攞老細著數啦！

A: 嘩！看看他一定是想找老闆便宜了！

B: For crying out loud! (explained in this book)

B: 唔該佢啦! 俾佢激死! (已經解釋咗 已經解釋了)

B: 氣死了！

Chapter 5

To Tease Somebody

攪笑嘅字

取笑人的詞

115. Cringe Cringe! – embarrassing - 好肉麻！/ 很肉麻！

e.g.SC: 2 friends watching a movie:

e.g.SC: 兩個朋友睇緊戲：

e.g.SC: 兩個朋友，正在看電影：

A: In the movie:

A: 喺戲度：

A: 在電影裏：

B: "Sandy – my love for you is deeper than the sea!"

B: 'Sandy，我對你嘅愛深過嗰海！'

B: 'Sandy，我對你的愛比海更深！'

A: turns to B: cringe cringe!!

A: 嘩！啲對白超肉麻喎！

A: 嘩！對白很肉麻啊！

B: I know – quite sickening!

B: 係啦！聽到毛管都戙晒！

B: 對啊！聽到毛孔都豎起來了！

e.g.SC: 2 good friends talking:

e.g.SC: 兩個好朋友講緊：

e.g.SC: 兩個好朋友在說：

A: So how did you propose to Sabrina?

A: 喂！咁你點向 Sabrina 求婚㗎？

A: 喂！那你怎樣向 Sabrina 求婚啊？

B: I just said, "Sabrina – you're the love of my life – I can't live without you!"

B: 我淨係話 'Sabrina，你係我一生最愛，我唔可以冇咗你㗎！'

B: 我只是說 'Sabrina，你是我一生最愛，我不可以沒有你的！'

A: Cringe cringe!! Did she say yes, then?

A: 嘩！肉麻爆呀！！咁佢有冇應承啫？

A: 嘩！很肉麻啊！！那她有沒有答應呢？

Raise the voice on the second '**surprise**!' to express surprise. 音調係第二個 surprise 到高音啲-表達驚喜 音調是在第二個 'surprise' 高音一些-表達驚喜

"**promises promises**!" empty words, not promises at all. 得嗰講字，吹水 空口講白話

e.g. A father and son

e.g. 老竇同嗰仔 爸爸和兒子

A (son): Dad, I know – I'll work harder next time.

A（仔）：老竇，我知！我下次會努力啲㗎喇！爸爸，我知道了！我下次會努力些的！

B (Dad): **Promises, promises**!

B（老竇）：得嗰講字啦你！

B: 你空口講白話！

"**surprise surprise**!" – sth you say when you give a surprise to sb. 驚喜

e.g. A husband and wife

e.g. 一對夫婦

A (husband) (holding a rose): Surprise, surprise darling! – it's our anniversary today!

A（老公）：（攞起支玫瑰）：驚喜嘛老婆？！今日係我哋結婚紀念日呀！（拿起玫瑰）：驚喜嗎老婆？！今天是我們結婚紀念日啊！

B (wife): How sweet of you!

B（老婆）：你真係好 sweet 嘅啫！

B: 你真是很 sweet 啊！

116. Nice one! / That was clever! – you've done it badly / wrongly, that's the reason it's gone wrong (satirical) - 抵你死啦！你都好叻啫！（諷刺）/ 你應得的！你死定了！你都很聰明！（諷刺）

e.g.SC: A has upset A's girlfriend:

e.g.SC: A 搞到佢女朋友唔開心：

e.g.SC: A 令到他女朋友不開心：

A: Mandy's dumped me!

A: Mandy 飛咗我呀！

A: Mandy 拋棄我啊！

B: Why?

B: 點解呀？

B: 為什麼？

A: I only said Sabrina looked nice today.

A: 我淨係話 Sabrina 今日扮得幾靚之嘛！

A: 我只是說 Sabrina 今天打扮得很漂亮而已！

B: Nice one! That's why she dumped you!

B: 抵你死啦！

B: 你應得的！

e.g.SC: 2 friends have just left the hotel they're staying at, to explore London, when the phone rings:

e.g.SC: 兩個朋友啱啱離開咗酒店，去 London 行吓。B 電話響：

e.g.SC: 兩個朋友剛剛離開了酒店，去 London 看一下。B 電話響了：

A: (person on the phone) …so what did you do with your iPad?

A: （喺電話度嗰人）……咁你部 iPad 呢？

A: （在電話中的人）……那你的 iPad 呢？

B: I left it in the hotel room. I didn't want to carry it around.

B: 我啲 iPad 擺低咗喺酒店喇！我唔想拎住佢周圍行囉！

B: 我留下了在酒店啊！我不想拿出去啊！

A: That was clever! You know it's quite rough in London. You shouldn't have left valuables in the room!

A: 喂，你都好叻啫！放貴重嘢喺間房度！你明知 London 幾雜㗎啦！

A: 你都很聰明啊！放一些貴重的東西在房間裏面！你明知道 London 是那麼混雜的！

B: Oh – it should be alright.

B: 噢！應該冇問題嘅！

B: 噢！應該沒有問題的！

Dumped me left me 拋棄我

To dump somebody – to end a relationship. 飛一個人, 拋棄一個人

rough in London = unsafe 不安全

117. Over the top, OTT – exaggeration - 誇張

e.g.SC: At a ball. A and B talking about someone's clothes:

e.g.SC: 喺 ball 場裏面，A 同 B 講緊另一個人嘅衫：

e.g.SC: 在 ball 場裏，A 和 B 說別人的衣服：

A: Hey, have a look at what she's wearing!

A: 嘩！你睇吓嗰個女人着成咁嘅！

A: 嘩！你看一下這個女人穿成怎麼樣？！

B: Wow! – that's just OTT!

B: 係呀！好鬼誇張呀！

B: 是啊！很誇張啊！

e.g.SC: At a Christmas party. A is commenting on a Christmas tree decoration:

e.g.SC: 喺 Xmas party，A 比緊意見關於棵聖誕樹嘅裝飾：

e.g.SC: 在 Xmas party，A 給一些意見，關於這棵聖誕樹的裝飾：

A: Wow! Look at this Christmas tree! There are tinsels and balls of all sizes and colours you can imagine!

A: 噢！睇吓棵聖誕樹！聖誕花條同聖誕波，咩 size 咩顏色都有喎！

A: 噢！看一下這棵聖誕樹！聖誕花條和聖誕波，什麼 size 什麼顏色都有啊！

B: Way too OTT! – too much of a good thing!

B: 太誇張喇！太多嘢喇！好睇都變，唔好睇啦！

B: 太誇張了！太多東西啊！好看都變成不好看了！

Too much of a good thing – sth becomes bad because there is too much of it 太多 - 好都變唔好 太多 - 好，都變成不好

118. Take the mickey (To take the mick) – to make fun of someone - 笑人，玩人/ 取笑人，玩弄人

e.g.SC: At a school year end dress up party, student B dresses up like the principal, who usually dresses in a funny way:

e.g.SC: 喺學校年度舞會，同學 B 扮到好似校長咁（校長平時着衫超古怪）：

e.g.SC: 在學校年度舞會中，同學 B 打扮到好像校長（校長日常穿着的衫都很古怪）：

A: Wow! Look at you! You look exactly like Mr. Redford!

A: 嘩！睇吓你？！真係搞笑！着到成個 Mr. Redford 咁！

A: 嘩！看一下你？！真是很好笑啊！穿着到好像 Mr. Redford 啊！

B: Just to take the mickey out of him!

B: 搞下笑啫！玩下佢吖嘛！

B: 真好笑啊！捉弄一下他而已！

e.g.SC: In a dance class. A tells B something which is untrue:

e.g.SC: 喺跳舞班裏邊，A 想玩 B：

e.g.SC: 在跳舞班裏面，A 想玩弄 B：

A: Hey, the instructor wants you to go to the front and demonstrate the steps!

A: 喂！導師想你去前邊示範俾我哋睇呀！

A: 喂！導師想你去前邊示範給我們看啊！

B: No way! – Are you taking the mick again?

B: 唔係下嘛，你又玩我喇！

B: 不會吧，你又捉弄我了！

To take the mickey /take the mick + out of sb

to pull somebody's leg - same meaning 取笑人

119. Wacky – (adj) funny, crazy - 搞笑，黐線 / 可笑的，瘋狂的

e.g.SC: At a dress-up party:

e.g.SC: 喺化妝舞會度：

e.g.SC: 在化妝舞會裏：

A: Look at Gordon! What a wacky outfit!

A: 嘩！你睇吓 Gordon！佢着得真係搞笑呀！

A: 嘩！你看吓 Gordon！他穿得真是可笑啊！

B: Whoa! Hilarious!

B: 嘩！真係好鬼搞笑喎！

B: 嘩！真是很滑稽了！

e.g.SC: In a staff canteen, A and B are talking:

e.g.SC: 喺員工 canteen 度，A 同 B 講：

e.g.SC: 在員工 canteen 裏，A 跟 B 說：

A: You always have wacky ideas! What's your latest?

A: 你成日有啲黐線嘅 idea！近排有咩巴閉野呀？

A: 你常常有些很瘋狂的想法！近來有沒有什麼了不起的東西啊？

B: Ahha! Trade secret!

B: 哈！商業秘密！

Hilarious (adj) – extremely funny e.g. a hilarious joke. 好搞笑嘅笑話 很滑稽的笑話

Amusing (adj) – funny and enjoyable e.g. an **amusing** movie 好得意套戲 很有趣的電影

To amuse (v) can also mean "to entertain" 娛樂

e.g. The children can amuse themselves for hours playing computer games.

e.g. 細路仔玩 PC game 嚟消磨時間同娛樂可以玩好幾個鐘。小孩子玩 PC game 來消磨時間和娛樂可以玩得好幾個小時。

120. Take the piss (out of someone) (rude) - to make a joke or make someone look silly – 同人開玩笑/ 令人出醜 (粗俗)

e.g.SC: 2 friends talking about someone else:

e.g.SC: 有兩個朋友，講緊第二個人啲嘢：

e.g.SC: 兩個朋友正在談論另外一個人：

A: Does Samuel still go to celebrities' fan clubs in this day and age?

A: 呀 Samuel 而家依個年代係咪仲去緊嗰啲 fans Club 呀？

A: Samuel 現在這個年代是否還去一些粉絲聚會啊？

B: Don't take the piss out of him when he's around- he'd be embarrassed!

B: 吓，如果佢喺度嗰陣時，千祈唔好笑佢呀，佢會好尷尬㗎！

B: 如果他在的時候，千萬不好笑他啊！他會很尷尬的！

e.g.SC: 2 friends are talking about a book they've been reading.

e.g.SC: 兩個朋友傾緊佢哋睇過一本書：

e.g.SC: 兩個朋友正在傾談他們讀過的書：

A: Have you finished it yet?

A: 你睇完未？

A: 你讀完沒有？

B: Yes, I have!

B: 係呀，我睇完喇！

B: 是啊！我讀完了！

A: What do you think the main point is?

A: 你覺得嗰 main point 係咩呀？

A: 你覺得這個重點是什麼啊？

B: The author is no doubt taking the piss out of the average salaryman.

B: 個作者一定係諷刺做藍領嗰啲人啦！

B: 這個作者一定是諷刺做文職的人吧！

Printed in Great Britain
by Amazon